GCSE Edexcel 360Science
Additional Science
Higher Workbook

This book is for anyone doing **GCSE Edexcel 360Science Additional Science** at higher level.

It's full of **tricky questions**... each one designed to make you **sweat** — because that's the only way you'll get any **better**.

There are questions to see **what facts** you know. There are questions to see how well you can **apply those facts**. And there are questions to see what you know about **how science works**.

It's also got some daft bits in to try and make the whole experience at least vaguely entertaining for you.

What CGP is all about

Our sole aim here at CGP is to produce the highest quality books — carefully written, immaculately presented and dangerously close to being funny.

Then we work our socks off to get them out to you — at the cheapest possible prices.

Contents

Published by Coordination Group Publications Ltd.

From original material by Paddy Gannon.

Editors:
Amy Boutal, Ellen Bowness, Katherine Craig, Sarah Hilton, Kate Houghton, Rose Parkin,
Ami Snelling, Laurence Stamford, Julie Wakeling, Sarah Williams.

Contributors:
Michael Aicken, Claire Charlton, Steve Coggins, Jane Davies, Ian H Davis, Catherine Debley,
Mark A Edwards, Dr Giles R Greenway, Max Fishel, James Foster, Dr Iona M J Hamilton,
Munir Kawar, Fred Langridge, Derek Harvey, Rebecca Harvey, Lucy Muncaster, John Myers,
Andy Rankin, Adrian Schmit, Claire Stebbing, Sidney Stringer Community School, Paul Warren,
Anna-Fe Williamson, Chris Workman.

ISBN: 978 1 84146 748 1

*With thanks to Barrie Crowther, Ian Francis, Sue Hocking and Glenn Rogers for the proofreading.
With thanks to Katie Steele for the copyright research.*

*Graph of percentage of waste recycled in England on page 35 from the e-digest environmental
statistics website: http://www.defra.gov.uk/environment/statistics. Crown Copyright material
is reproduced with the permission of the Controller of HMSO.*

*Graph of cod and herring stocks on page 39 from www.statistics.gov.uk. Crown Copyright
material reproduced with the permission of the Controller of HMSO.*

*Graph of global temperature variation on page 43 reproduced with permission of the Climatic
Research Unit, School of Environmental Sciences, University of East Anglia: www.cru.uea.ac.uk.*

*Data to construct graph on page 51 is from Defra and is reproduced under the terms of the
Click-Use Licence.*

Groovy website: www.cgpbooks.co.uk

Printed by Elanders Hindson Ltd, Newcastle upon Tyne.
Jolly bits of clipart from CorelDRAW®

Respiration

Q1   Part of the **word equation** for one type of **respiration** is shown below.

    a)   Complete the equation for respiration.

> .... + oxygen → carbon dioxide + ... + ...

    b)   What type of respiration is this? ....

Q2   Which of these statements is **not** true of respiration? Underline the correct answer.

It takes place in every cell of your body.

It releases energy from food.

It is another word for breathing.

It can be aerobic or anaerobic.

Q3   Give three things that the body uses the **energy** obtained in respiration for.

....

....

Q4   Draw lines to match the **body part** or **process** to the correct description.

capillaries	The system that provides the food source needed for respiration.
circulatory system	The gradual movement of particles from areas of higher concentration to areas of lower concentration.
diffusion	The smallest blood vessels that carry blood to all body cells.
digestive system	The system that carries substances like glucose, oxygen and carbon dioxide around your body.

Q5   The diagram shows **blood** passing through **muscle tissue**.

    a)   On the diagram, draw labelled arrows to show whether **oxygen (O_2)**, **glucose (G)** and **carbon dioxide (CO_2)** move **into** or **out of** the muscle cells.

    b)   Explain how these substances move into and out of the blood in terms of concentration gradients.

muscle cells

blood capillary

direction of blood flow

....

....

....

....

<u>Respiration and Exercise</u>

Q1 Jim is a keen runner. He takes part in a 400 metre race. The **graph** below shows Jim's **breathing rate** before, during and after the race.

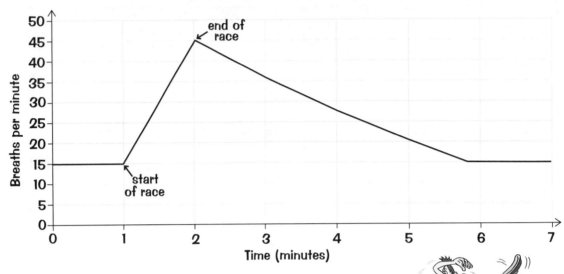

a) How much does Jim's breathing rate go up during the race?

.......30.......... **breaths per minute**

b) Explain why exercise makes Jim's breathing rate increase.

The muscles are being used in the body. They require oxygen to function. The heart then has to pump blood faster around the body so the blood cells can carry the oxygen to the muscles. This is how the breathing rate increases.

c) Why **doesn't** Jim's breathing rate return to normal immediately after the race?

Think about the products of anaerobic respiration.

Because it takes time for the heart to go back to normal rate. The muscles cool down in the body.

Q2 Amy used a **digital monitor** to measure how her body changed during exercise.

a) What three things could Amy monitor?

Heat, pulse rate, breathing rate

b) The monitor allowed Amy to continuously record the changes that happened to her body. Give two other advantages of using digital monitors.

More reliable, able to measure factors that you can't measure manually.

Respiration and Exercise

Q3 Humans can respire **aerobically** — if there isn't enough oxygen available we can also respire **anaerobically**.

a) Give **two** advantages of aerobic respiration over anaerobic respiration.

1. *uses oxygen to release energy and produces carbon dioxide*

2. *Complete Conversion of oxygen and to carbon dioxide*

b) In what circumstances would a human start respiring anaerobically?

The absence of oxygen when exercising and your not breaking down gucose completely

c) Mary-Kate doesn't like sport and is unfit. Ashley is sporty and on the county hockey team. Both girls run an 800 m race. Which girl will start respiring **anaerobically** first?

Mary-Kate

d) Write the **word equation** for anaerobic respiration in humans.

Glucose → Energy + Lactic acid

Q4 Roy wants to find out which of his friends has the shortest 'recovery' time. Your recovery time is how long it takes for your pulse rate to **return to normal** after exercise. Roy tests each of his friends separately. He measures their **pulse rate**, then asks them to **run** for 2 minutes. After they've finished running, he measures their pulse rate at 15 second intervals until it has returned to normal.

a) Write down **two** things Roy should do to ensure it is a **fair test**.

Think about keeping things constant.

1. *using a stop watch or clock to make sure it is 15 seconds each interval*

2.

b) Here is a sketch of Roy's results. Which of his friends had the **shortest** recovery time?

Jim

Pulse rate

KEY
—Jim
—Saeed
—Bonnie

Time

Evaluating Health Claims

Q1 Two reports on **low-fat foods** were published on one day. **Report A** appeared in a tabloid paper. It said that the manufacturers of 'Chewy Bites' have shown that the latest girl band, Kandyfloss, lost weight using their product. **Report B** appeared in the *Journal of Medicine* and reported how 6000 volunteers lost weight during a trial of an experimental drug.

Which of these reports is likely to be the most reliable and why?

....

....

....

Q2 Three **weight loss methods** appeared in the headlines last week.

(1) **Hollywood star swears carrot soup aids weight loss**

(2) **Survey of 10 000 dieters shows it's exercise that counts**

(3) **Atkins works! 5000 in study lose weight... but what about their health?**

a) Which of these headlines are more likely to refer to **scientific studies**? Explain your answer.

③ because it shows a detailed opinion and shows it considers other factors.

b) Why might following the latest celebrity diet not always help you lose weight?

....

....

Q3 **Statins** are drugs that lower the levels of 'bad' cholesterol in the blood. A drug trial to test their effectiveness involved 6000 patients with **high cholesterol levels**. 3000 patients were given statins and 3000 were not. Both groups were advised to make lifestyle changes to lower their cholesterol. The decrease in their cholesterol levels compared to their levels at the start is shown on the graph.

a) Why was the group without statins included?

....

b) Suggest a conclusion that can be drawn from these results.

....

....

B2 Topic 1 — Inside Living Cells

Evaluating Health Claims

Q4   The **UK government** has a responsibility to educate the public about how to have a **healthy diet**.

FOOD	MORE	LESS
Fruit		
Salt		
Sugars		
Oily fish		
Vegetables		
Fat		

a)   The advice the government provides suggests that most people need to cut their intake of some foods and to try to eat more of others.

Tick the boxes in the table on the right to show how you think the average person in the UK should adjust their diet to conform to government advice.

b)   Name **two** organisations that provide the government with evidence to support the advice that they give.

1. ....

2. ....

Q5   After Amanda's father died of **heart disease**, she decided to record the amount of **exercise** she did, to see if it was enough to reduce her risk of heart disease. On the right is her exercise diary for one week.

DAY	ACTIVITY
Sunday	Run with the dog, 10 minutes.
Monday	Run with the dog, 10 minutes.
Tuesday	Run with the dog, 10 minutes, Swim 20 minutes.
Wednesday	Run with the dog, 10 minutes.
Thursday	Run with the dog, 10 minutes.
Friday	Run with the dog, 10 minutes, Swim 20 minutes.
Saturday	Run with the dog, 10 minutes.

a)   What is the total time Amanda spent exercising last week?

....

b)   What is the current UK government recommendation for the amount of exercise a person should do each week? Give your answer in **minutes per week**.

....

c)   What is the difference between this total and Amanda's total?

....

d)   Until quite recently, the amount of exercise recommended by the government was lower than the current recommendation. Explain why the advice changed.

....

....

....

Top Tips: The overall message here is **don't believe everything you read**. You have to carry out proper trials, with a large sample size, scientists who know what they're doing, and a method that ensures a fair comparison, before you can begin to suggest that something is good or bad for you.

B2 Topic 1 — Inside Living Cells

DNA — Making Proteins

Q1 The following questions are about **DNA**.

a) What is the function of DNA?

....

b) What name is given to the shape of a DNA molecule? ....

c) How many different bases make up the DNA structure? ....

d) Which bases pair up together?

....

Q2 Tick the boxes to show whether the following statements are **true** or **false**.

		True	False
a)	Genes are sections of DNA that code for specific proteins.	☐	☐
b)	Each amino acid is coded for by a set of four base pairs.	☐	☐
c)	Each cell contains different genes, which is why we have different types of cell.	☐	☐
d)	Proteins are made by ribosomes.	☐	☐
e)	RNA is a messenger molecule that communicates between DNA and the ribosomes.	☐	☐
f)	RNA contains two strands, like DNA.	☐	☐

Q3 Answer the following questions to explain how a section of code on a **DNA molecule** can be used to build a new **protein**.

a) How is a molecule of messenger RNA formed from a molecule of DNA?

....

....

b) How do RNA and ribosomes work together to build proteins?

....

....

Q4 On the section of **DNA** shown:

A G G C T A G C C A A T C G C C G A A G C T C A

T C C G A T C G G T T A G C G

a) Complete the lower sequence of bases.

b) Calculate how many amino acids are coded for by this section of DNA.

....

Using Microorganisms

Q1 Circle the correct word in each pair to complete the sentences below.

> Microorganisms use photosynthesis / respiration to release energy / oxygen from sugars / salts.
>
> If this process is anaerobic it is also known as distillation / fermentation.

Q2 Some microorganisms can respire **aerobically** or **anaerobically**.

  a) What is the difference between aerobic and anaerobic respiration?

  ....

  b) How is aerobic respiration used in the process of breadmaking?

  ....

  ....

Q3 Number the following stages in the process of **making cheese** to put them into the correct order.

  .... An increased acidity of the milk causes curdling.

  .... Lactose is converted into lactic acid by the bacteria.

  .... The curdles are compressed into cheese.

  .... Bacteria are placed into milk.

  .... The milk becomes more acidic.

  .... The bacteria feed on the milk, which contains a sugar called lactose.

Q4 Sarah has been diagnosed with **type 1 diabetes**. She has been told that she needs to have daily injections of a **hormone**.

  a) What is the name of this hormone? ....

  b) Give **two** reasons why it's better for diabetics to use hormones produced by microorganisms than hormones from animals such as pigs.

  1. ....

  2. ....

Top Tips: Bacteria aren't the only things that can respire anaerobically — if you hold both arms out from your sides for as long as you can, your shoulders start to burn. That's because your muscles start respiring anaerobically, producing lactic acid, which causes the pain... Nice.

B2 Topic 1 — Inside Living Cells

Using Microorganisms

Q5   The diagram below shows a **fermenter** that can be used for producing **mycoprotein**.

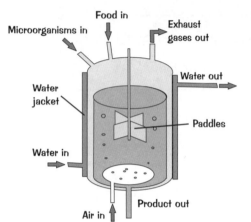

a)   Explain the purpose of each of the following:

    i)   the water jacket

....

    ii)   the air supply

....

    iii) the paddles

....

b)   Before fermentation begins, the fermenter is usually filled with steam and then cooled. Why is this done?

....

c)   What is mycoprotein used for?

....

Q6 a)   Match the descriptions below to the different stages of insulin production by putting the correct letter next to the diagram.

    A   The hormone produced by the bacteria is purified and can then be used as a treatment.

    B   The bacteria are cultivated until millions of identical bacteria have grown.

    C   Another enzyme cuts the bacterial DNA so that the human section of DNA can be inserted.

    D   A human DNA sample is taken.

    E   Enzymes are used to cut the human insulin gene from the human DNA.

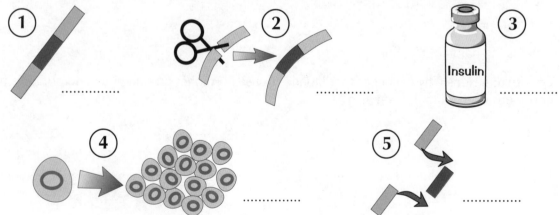

b)   Arrange the numbers to give the steps in the correct order.

....

Using Microorganisms

Q7 Circle the correct word in each pair to complete the passage below.

Some bacteria / viruses that cause disease can be killed or stopped from growing by
hormones / antibiotics. These are produced by other microorganisms — for example,
insulin / penicillin is produced by a virus / mould. This mould can be grown in a fermenter
using a liquid / solid culture medium that contains starch / sugars and nitrates / sodium.

Q8 Give three advantages of producing **foods** using **microorganisms** rather than other organisms.

1. ....

2. ....

3. ....

Q9 A group of students set up the experiment below to simulate the conditions in a **fermenter**.

1. **Make up the culture medium and put it into a sterile flask.**

2. **Add a sample of the microorganism (yeast).**

3. **Seal the flask with a ventilated bung that lets gas out but not in.**

4. **Mix thoroughly then place in the incubator at 37 °C.**

5. **Remove from the incubator for mixing every 15 minutes.**

a) Name three substances that a culture medium would usually contain.

....

b) George set up his experiment but forgot to put the flask into the incubator.
What effect would this have on his experiment?

....

c) Give one reason why the contents of the flask needed to be mixed regularly.

....

d) The teacher asked pupils to take a small sample of their culture medium and test it
with Universal Indicator paper. Why did they need to do this?

....

e) Do you think that the yeast cells were respiring aerobically or anaerobically? Explain your answer.

....

B2 Topic 2 — Divide and Develop

Growth in Organisms

Q1 If an organism increases in size or weight, it is **growing**.

a) Give one way to measure the **size** of an organism.

....

b) How do you measure the **dry weight** of an organism?

....

Q2 A Year 10 class investigated the **heights** of the class members. The results are shown on the graph.

a) What type of variation did they investigate? Circle your choice.

Continuous / Discontinuous

b) What was the **shortest** height in the group?

....

c) What was the **tallest** height in the group?

....

d) Into what range of heights did most pupils fall? Circle your choice.

| 141–150 cm | 151–160 cm | 161–170 cm |

e) Give three things that influence height in humans.

1. .... 2. .... 3. ....

Q3 Some animals can **regenerate** parts of their bodies.

a) What does 'regenerate' mean?

....

b) Give an example of regeneration.

....

Q4 **Growth factors** are naturally produced in the bodies of animals.

a) What are growth factors?

....

b) Why is it illegal for athletes to take growth factor drugs?

....

c) Give **two** possible side effects of using growth factor drugs.

....

Cell Division — Mitosis

Q1 Decide whether the following statements are **true** or **false**.

		True	False
a)	Human body cells are diploid.	☐	☐
b)	There are 20 pairs of chromosomes in a human cheek cell.	☐	☐
c)	Chromosomes are found in the cytoplasm of a cell.	☐	☐
d)	Before a cell divides by mitosis, it duplicates its DNA.	☐	☐
e)	Mitosis is where a cell splits to create two genetically identical copies.	☐	☐
f)	Each new cell produced in mitosis gets one chromosome from each pair.	☐	☐
g)	Organisms use mitosis in order to grow.	☐	☐
h)	Organisms do not use mitosis to replace damaged cells.	☐	☐

Q2 The following diagram shows the different stages of **mitosis**.
Write a short description to explain each stage.

a) ....

b) ....

c) ....
....

d) ....
....

e) ....

Q3 Write a definition of the **Hayflick limit** for a science dictionary. Include in your definition the
Hayflick limit for most **human cells** and examples of two cell types that have **no** Hayflick limit.

....
....
....

Cell Division — Meiosis

Q1 Tick the boxes to show if each statement is true of **mitosis**, **meiosis** or **both**.

	Mitosis	Meiosis
a) Gives new cells that each have half the original number of chromosomes.	☐	☐
b) The chromosomes line up in the centre of the cell.	☐	☐
c) Forms cells that are genetically identical.	☐	☐
d) In humans, this only happens in the reproductive organs.	☐	☐

Q2 Draw lines to match each description of the stage of **meiosis** to the right diagram below.

a)

b)

c)

d)

e)

The pairs are pulled apart, mixing up the mother and father's chromosomes into the new cells. This creates genetic variation.

Before the cell starts to divide it duplicates its DNA to produce an exact copy.

There are now 4 gametes, each containing half the original number of chromosomes.

For the first meiotic division the chromosomes line up in their pairs across the centre of the cell.

The chromosomes line up across the centre of the nucleus ready for the second division, and the two arms of each chromosome are pulled apart.

Q3 During sexual reproduction, two **gametes** combine to form a new individual.

a) What are gametes? ....

b) Explain why gametes have half the usual number of chromosomes.

....

....

c) Explain how meiotic cell division gives rise to genetic variation.

....

....

Top Tips: It's easy to get confused between **mitosis** and **meiosis**. Mitosis produces cells for growth and replaces damaged cells. Meiosis is for sexual reproduction and creates gametes.

Stem Cells and Differentiation

Q1 Tick the correct boxes to show whether the following statements are **true** or **false**.

		True	False
a)	Cells in an early embryo are unspecialised.	☐	☐
b)	Blood cells are undifferentiated.	☐	☐
c)	Nerve cells are specialised cells.	☐	☐
d)	Adult stem cells are as versatile as embryonic stem cells.	☐	☐
e)	Stem cells in bone marrow can differentiate into any type of cell.	☐	☐

Q2 Scientists in the UK are carrying out research into the use of stem cells in **medicine**.

a) Describe one way in which stem cells are **already** used in medicine.

....

b) Describe how it might be possible to use embryonic stem cells to treat disease in the future.

....

....

Q3 People have **different opinions** when it comes to embryonic **stem cell research**.

a) Give one argument **in favour** of stem cell research. ....

....

b) Give one argument **against** stem cell research. ....

....

Q4 It is illegal to **terminate pregnancies** in the UK after the foetus is a certain age.

a) What is this age in weeks? ....

b) Explain why the limit was set at this particular stage of pregnancy.

....

....

c) Give two situations in which an abortion may be allowed after this limit has passed.

....

....

d) Explain why some people feel that abortion is unethical.

....

....

__Growth in Plants__

Q1   Green plants were grown in a lab to investigate the effect of **mineral deficiency** on plant growth.

a)   Plant A had yellow leaves. Which mineral was in short supply? ....

b)   Plant B was grown in a solution low in nitrates. What effect would this have?

....

c)   Why would a plant grown in a solution low in phosphates have poor growth?

....

Q2   Michelle put her baby's paddling pool on the lawn. The sunny weather made the grass around the pool **grow quickly**, but when Michelle moved the pool she found that the grass under it had **died**. Explain why.

....

....

Q3   Nick had heard that plants grow better when they are **warm**. He put his favourite plant on top of a hot radiator and kept it well watered, but the plant **died**.

a)   Why do plants grow better when they are warm?

....

b)   Explain why Nick's plant died.

....

....

Q4   Why do plants need:

a)   Carbon dioxide? ....

b)   Oxygen? ....

Q5   Rory carried out an investigation into the **distribution** of marram grass in an area between the shoreline and dense forest. His results are shown in the graph below.

a)   Describe the distribution of marram grass.

....

....

b)   Suggest a reason for this distribution.

....

....

Growth in Plants: Plant Hormones

Q1 Three **plant shoots** were set up with a **light stimulus**.
The diagram shows the shape of each shoot before and after.

a) Which part of the plant shoot is most sensitive to light?

....

b) Which plant hormone controls the growth of the tip?

....

c) On each picture, shade in the region that
contains the most of this hormone.

Q2 Growth hormones can change the **direction** in which shoots and roots grow.

a) Complete the diagrams below to show which way the root or shoot **will grow** and explain your
answer with reference to growth hormones.

i)   Explanation:

....

....

ii) Explanation:

....

....

iii) Explanation:

....

....

b) Explain why these different responses are important in the survival of the seedling.

....

....

Q3 Erica bought a **seedless satsuma** to school and asked her teacher why it contained no seeds.

a) How do fruits (with seeds) normally develop?

....

b) Explain how seedless citrus fruits are grown.

....

....

Selective Breeding

Q1 Circle the correct word(s) in each pair to complete the passage below.

> Selective breeding leads to less variety / DNA in the gene pool of a population.
>
> All of the organisms in the population will be sterile / closely related.
>
> This means that they will have similar / different characteristics.
>
> That can be an advantage, e.g. if they all have high temperatures / milk yields.
>
> However, it can also be a disadvantage, e.g. if they are all resistant / susceptible
>
> to the same disease.

Q2 Garfield wants to breed one type of plant for its **fruit**, and another as an **ornamental house plant**.

a) Suggest **two** characteristics that he should select for in each kind of plant.

Fruit plant: 1. ....

2. ....

Ornamental house plant: 1. ....

2. ....

b) Why is selective breeding also called 'artificial' selection?

....

....

Q3 Some breeds of **sheep** have been bred for their high level of **fertility**.

a) Describe how selective breeding from a sheep stock with **low fertility** could produce a breed that has a **higher number of offspring**.

....

....

b) Explain why some farmed sheep breeds are likely to suffer from genetic disorders.

....

....

Many genetic disorders are recessive, i.e. you have to have two copies of the same faulty allele before you develop the condition.

....

....

Selective Breeding

Q4 The graph shows the **milk yield** for a population of cows over three generations.

a) Do you think that selective breeding is likely to have been used with these cows? Explain your answer.

....

....

b) What is the increase in the average milk yield per cow from generation 1 to generation 2?

....

c) What is the smallest milk yield recorded for generation 3?

....

d) Suggest why the milk yield will reach a maximum limit after many generations.

....

Key: Generation 1 ——
Generation 2 ——
Generation 3 ——

Number of cows

Milk yield / litres produced per year per cow

Q5 The red **jungle fowl** is thought to be the wild ancestor of all farm-bred chickens. Farm-bred chickens have been produced by **selective breeding** for egg laying.

a) Suggest three ways in which farm-bred chickens are likely to differ from wild red jungle fowls.

....

....

b) Suggest how selective breeding in chickens might harm the welfare of the birds.

....

....

Q6 There are two varieties of **wheat plants** that have the characteristics outlined below:

WHEAT PLANT	GRAIN YIELD	RESISTANCE TO BAD WEATHER
Tall plant	High	Low
Dwarf plant	Low	High

How could a wheat plant be created with a **high yield** and **high resistance** to bad weather?

....

....

B2 Topic 2 — Divide and Develop

Cloning and Genetic Modification

Q1   **Dolly the sheep** was born in 1996.

   a)   Explain why the birth of this lamb was so significant from a scientific point of view.

....

   b)   Describe the process that was used to create Dolly the sheep.

....

....

....

Q2   In nature, cloning involves a single parent, but the procedure used to create
Dolly the sheep involved **three 'parents'** as outlined in the table below.

Parent	Involvement in creating Dolly
1	Provided the egg cell
2	Provided the diploid nucleus
3	Embryo implanted into the uterus

Dolly was genetically identical to only one of her three 'parents'. Which parent was this?
Explain your answer.

....

....

Q3   Describe the **disadvantages** of cloning, in relation to:

   a)   Success rate   ....

....

   b)   Genetic defects   ....

....

   c)   The immune system   ....

....

Top Tips: Poor Dolly had to be put down (aged six) due to lung disease — that's only **half** the
age sheep of her breed can reach. They're not sure if it was due to her being a **clone**, but it's certainly
true that clones tend to suffer **health problems**.

Cloning and Genetic Modification

Q4 Answer the following questions about **genetic modification**.

a) What does genetic modification mean?

....

....

b) At which point in its life cycle should an organism be genetically modified?

....

c) Explain how genetic modification could be of use in treating genetic disorders.

....

....

Q5 Explain why some people are **concerned** about genetic modification.

....

....

....

Q6 **Pyrethrum** is an **insecticide**. It is found naturally in chrysanthemum plants.

a) A gene to make pyrethrum could be used to improve the pest resistance of soya plants. Put these stages in order to show how this could be done:

A	Soya plants display pest resistance.
B	Identify the pyrethrum gene.
C	Insert the gene into the DNA of a soya plant.
D	Extract the gene from the chrysanthemum DNA.

Order: ...., ..., ..., ...

b) Give one advantage and one disadvantage of producing GM soya in this way.

....

....

....

Gene Therapy

Q1   Genes code for **proteins** in the body. Inherited disorders
are the result of inheriting a **faulty copy** of a gene.

   a)   What happens to the protein if the gene is faulty?

....

   b)   Give the name of a disease or disorder caused by:

      i)   A single faulty gene. ....

      ii)   A combination of inherited genes and environmental factors. ....

Q2   It is hoped that **gene therapy** may be useful in treating genetic disorders.

   a)   What is gene therapy?

....

....

   b)   Outline the problems associated with gene therapy.

....

....

Q3   Decide whether each of the following statements is **true** or **false**.

		True	False
a)	Gene therapy involves inserting functional versions of faulty proteins into cells.	☐	☐
b)	Some people have genes that make them more likely to get cancer.	☐	☐
c)	Suicide genes are used to attack the cells that cause cystic fibrosis.	☐	☐
d)	Some scientists worry that suicide genes could be taken up by healthy cells.	☐	☐
e)	In the UK, embryos at risk of inheriting diseases are genetically modified.	☐	☐
f)	Gene therapy would prevent diseases being passed on to the next generation.	☐	☐

Q4   It is hoped that gene therapy could one day be used to treat **cancer**.

Outline one possible method that could be used to treat cancer with gene therapy.

....

....

....

Mixed Questions — B2 Topics 1 & 2

Q1 The **Large White** is a breed of pig that is farmed for meat. Large Whites can tolerate harsh weather, and the females are good mothers that produce a lot of offspring. **Selective breeding** from wild pigs has produced the Large White.

a) Choose one of the features of the Large White and suggest how this is an advantage in farming.

....

b) Explain how the characteristics above would have been produced through selective breeding.

....

....

c) If a **gene** that caused Large Whites to produce particularly large litters of offspring was isolated, how might this be used to improve the litter sizes of another species?

....

....

d) A farmer breeds a pig that lives for an unexpectedly long time. It remains healthy and produces many more litters during its lifetime than the average pig. He decides to clone it to reproduce these useful features exactly. Explain why this may not have the desired effect.

....

....

Q2 Several students **germinated beans**. When the beans had germinated, they turned them sideways so that the roots and shoots were **horizontal**. The results after three days are shown below.

a) Name the hormones responsible for these changes.

....

start — bean, shoot, root

3 days later — bean, shoot, root

b) Explain the results observed.

....

....

c) Give **three** other factors that affect the **growth** and **distribution** of plants.

1. ....

2. ....

3. ....

Mixed Questions — B2 Topics 1 & 2

Q3 Humans can respire **aerobically** and **anaerobically**.

a) Give a definition of respiration, including where it happens in the body.

....

b) Complete the following sentences about anaerobic respiration in humans.

Anaerobic respiration is respiration without ....

A waste product, ..., is produced. ....

energy is released during anaerobic respiration than during aerobic respiration.

c) Anaerobic respiration is not as efficient as aerobic respiration. Why is it still useful to us?

....

....

d) Some **bacteria** can respire anaerobically.
Explain how certain anaerobic bacteria can be useful in cheese making.

....

....

Q4 Two studies into the **Atkins diet** were published in the New England Journal of Medicine in 2003. The first tested 132 obese patients, and the second tested 63 patients. Both concluded that patients on the Atkins diet lost slightly **more** weight than patients on a conventional low-fat diet.

a) Give three reasons why this is likely to be a trustworthy conclusion.

1. ....

2. ....

3. ....

b) Both these studies noted that longer and larger studies were still needed to determine the long-term safety of the Atkins diet.

Explain why the UK government does **not** recommend Atkins as part of a healthy diet.

....

....

Q5 **Useful genes** can be transferred into plants and animals at an early stage in their development. Outline **one** use of this technique.

....

....

Mixed Questions — B2 Topics 1 & 2

Q6 One way that organisms **grow** is by making new cells by **mitosis**.

The graph shows how the amount of DNA per cell changes as a cell undergoes two cell divisions by mitosis. Point C on the graph is the time when the chromosomes first become visible in the new cells.

a) Describe and explain what is happening to the DNA during stage A.

....

....

b) Describe another change happening in the cell during this stage.

....

c) What happens at time B?

....

Q7 In the future **gene therapy** could be used to treat genetic disorders such as **cystic fibrosis** (CF). John is CF sufferer. He and his wife Mary are planning to start a family.

a) If John could be successfully treated with gene therapy for cystic fibrosis, why would his children still be at risk of inheriting the faulty version of the gene?

....

....

....

b) If Mary was a carrier, how could John and Mary be sure of having a child without the faulty CF gene?

....

....

Q8 Young spiders that lose a leg can **grow** another one — this type of growth is called **regeneration**.

a) Young spiders contain a lot of **stem cells**. Explain why stem cells are needed for regeneration.

....

b) Adult spiders are **not** able to regenerate lost body parts. Suggest a reason for this.

....

Mixed Questions — B2 Topics 1 & 2

Q9 Mosquitoes have **three pairs** of **chromosomes** in their body cells. The diagram shows a cell from a mosquito which is about to divide by **meiosis**.

a) Below, draw the chromosomes in one of the cells produced from this cell:

i) after the first division stage of meiosis.

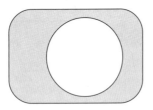

ii) after the second division stage of meiosis.

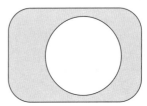

b) Describe what happens to the chromosomes at the following stages:

i) the first meiotic division. ....

....

ii) the second meiotic division. ....

....

Q10 **Proteins** are large molecules coded for by **DNA**.

a) Explain how each of the following are involved in building **new proteins**.

i) Genes ....

ii) Free amino acids ....

iii) Base triplets ....

iv) RNA ....

v) Ribosomes ....

b) Some **human diseases** are caused by a **lack** of a **working protein**, e.g. people with type 1 diabetes don't produce enough of the protein insulin or don't produce any at all.
Describe how microorganisms are used to treat diabetes.

....

....

....

Q11 Circle the correct word from each pair to complete the passage below.

The climate in some countries makes it hard to farm animals. Because animals are an important source of protein / fibre, an alternative is needed. Mycoprotein / Penicillin is one possibility. This is obtained from a bacteria / fungus that respires anaerobically / aerobically. Microorganisms grow more slowly / quickly than animals, they are easy to look after, and some can use waste / heat as a source of food.

B2 Topic 2 — Divide and Develop

Plants and Photosynthesis

Q1 Plant and animal cells have **similarities** and **differences**.
Complete each statement below by circling the correct words.

a) Plant / Animal cells, but not plant / animal cells, contain chloroplasts.

b) Plant cells have vacuoles / cytoplasm containing cell sap.

c) Both plant and animal cells / Only plant cells / Only animal cells have cell membranes.

d) Chloroplasts are where respiration / photosynthesis occurs, which makes glucose / water.

Q2 This question is about the **content** and **function** of cellular structures.

a) State what each of the following cell structures contains or is made of.

i) The **nucleus** contains ....

ii) **Chloroplasts** contain ....

iii) The **cell wall** is made of ....

b) Explain the function of these cellular structures.

i) The **nucleus** ....

ii) **Chloroplasts** ....

iii) The **cell wall** ....

Q3 **Photosynthesis** is the process that produces 'food' in plants.
Use some of the words below to complete the equation for photosynthesis.

oxygen   carbon dioxide   nitrogen   water   glucose   sodium chloride

$$\text{.................} + \text{.................} \xrightarrow[\text{chlorophyll}]{\text{sunlight}} \text{.................} + \text{.................}$$

Q4 Decide whether each of the following statements is **true** or **false**.

		True	False
a)	Photosynthesis happens inside the chloroplasts.	☐	☐
b)	Photosynthesis happens in all plant cells.	☐	☐
c)	Plants absorb carbon dioxide from the air.	☐	☐
d)	Plant cells don't respire.	☐	☐
e)	Sunlight provides the energy for photosynthesis.	☐	☐

Q5 Humans use a lot of plants as **food**, but also use materials produced by plants in other ways. Give three ways in which **plant materials** are used (apart from as food) and include an **example** of each.

....

....

....

Rate of Photosynthesis

Q1 Define the term **'limiting factor'**.

....

Q2 Seth investigated the effect of different concentrations of **carbon dioxide** on the rate of photosynthesis of his Swiss cheese plant. The results are shown on the graph below.

a) Describe the effect on the rate of photosynthesis of increasing the concentration of CO_2.

....

....

....

Key:
- 0.4% CO_2
- 0.1% CO_2
- 0.04% CO_2

b) Explain why all the lines level off eventually.

....

....

Think about other limiting factors.

Q3 **Average summer temperatures** in different habitats around the world are recorded in the table below.

Habitat	Temperature (°C)
Forest	19
Arctic	0
Desert	32
Grassland	22
Rainforest	27

a) Plot a **bar chart** for these results on the grid.

b) From the values for temperature, in which area would you expect the fewest plants to grow?

....

c) Suggest a reason for your answer above using the terms **enzymes** and **photosynthesis**.

....

....

d) Explain why very few plants can grow in the desert even though it has a much higher average temperature than the rainforest where many varieties of plants can grow.

....

....

Rate of Photosynthesis

Q4   Lucy investigated the **volume of oxygen** produced by pondweed at **different intensities of light**. Her results are shown in the table below.

Relative light intensity	1	2	3	4	5
Volume of oxygen produced in 10 minutes (ml)	12	25	13	48	61

bubbles of oxygen

pondweed

a)   What did Lucy measure by recording the volume of oxygen produced?

....

b)   Plot a graph of her results.

c)   **i)**   One of Lucy's results is anomalous. Circle this point on the graph.

   ii)   Suggest an error Lucy might have made when she collected this result.

      ....

      ....

      ....

d)   Describe the relationship shown on the graph between light intensity and photosynthesis rate.

   ....

....

e)   Would you expect this relationship to continue if Lucy continued to increase the light intensity? Explain your answer.

....

....

Q5   Farmer Fred doesn't put his cows out during the winter because the grass is **not growing**.

a)   Give **two** differences between summer and winter conditions that affect the rate of photosynthesis.

   1. ....

   2. ....

b)   How are the rate of photosynthesis and the growth rate of the grass related?

....

....

The Carbon Cycle

Q1   Complete the diagram below as instructed to show a **part** of the **carbon cycle**.

CO_2 in the air

plant   animal

a)   Add an arrow or arrows labelled **P** to represent **photosynthesis**.

b)   Add an arrow or arrows labelled **R** to represent **respiration**.

c)   Add an arrow or arrows labelled **F** to represent **feeding**.

Q2   Answer the following questions to show how the **stages** in the **carbon cycle** are ordered.

a)   Number the sentences below to show how carbon moves between the air and living things.

.... Animals eat the plants' carbon compounds.

....**1**.... Carbon dioxide in the air.

.... Plants and animals die.

.... Plants take in carbon dioxide for photosynthesis and make carbon compounds.

b)   Add a point 5 to complete the cycle and show how carbon in dead organisms is returned to the air.

Point 5: ....

Q3   Answer the following questions about the **carbon cycle**.

a)   What is the most common form of carbon found in the atmosphere?

    ....

b)   What products do plants convert this carbon into?

    ....

c)   How is the carbon in plants passed on through the food chain?

    ....

d)   Give three things that can happen to dead plants and animals.

    1. ....

    2. ....

    3. ....

The Carbon Cycle

Q4   The diagram below shows one version of the **carbon cycle**.

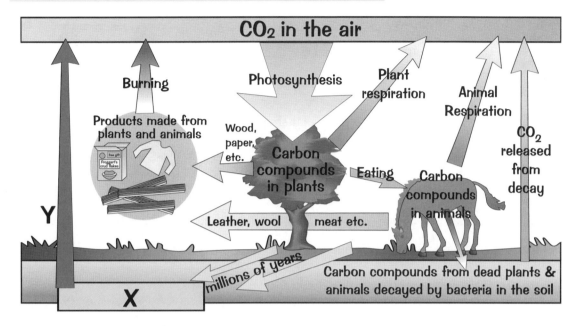

a)   Name substance **X** shown on the diagram above. ....

b)   Explain why substance **X** contains carbon.

....

....

c)   Name the process labelled **Y** on the diagram above. ....

Q5   Nutrients are constantly **recycled**.

a)   Name **three** elements (other than carbon) that are recycled in the environment.

....

b)   Explain why **microorganisms** are important in recycling nutrients.

Don't just describe what the microorganisms do — explain why it's important.

....

....

....

Top Tip: Lots of substances are **recycled**, not just carbon. They enter organisms when they feed (or photosynthesise) and leave when they die, breathe or poo. That's the great circle of life for you.

Minerals and Plants

Q1   A diagram of a **specialised plant cell** is shown on the right.

a)   Name the type of cell shown. ....

b)   What is the main function of this type of cell?

....

c)   Why does this type of cell have the particular shape shown in the diagram?

....

d)   What do plants use phosphates for?

....

e)   Explain why minerals are **not** absorbed from the soil by the process of diffusion.

....

....

f)   Explain how these specialised cells absorb minerals from the soil.
Use the words **active transport**, **concentration**, **respiration** and **energy** in your answer.

....

....

Q2   Rivers and lakes can be **polluted** by **fertilisers** that come from
nearby farmland. This often results in the death of many fish.

a)   Why are fertilisers essential to modern farming?

....

b)   How does the fertiliser get into the rivers and lakes?

....

c)   How does pollution by fertilisers cause fish to die?

....

....

d)   What is the name given to this type of pollution by fertilisers? ....

e)   What can farmers do to avoid causing this type of pollution?

....

....

The Nitrogen Cycle

Q1   Circle the correct word to complete each statement below.

a)   Nitrogen is need to make protein / carbohydrate / fat.

b)   The percentage of nitrogen in the **air** is **94%** / **21%** / **78%**.

c)   Nitrogen is **a reactive gas** / **an unreactive gas** / **a reactive liquid**.

Q2   Match up each type of **organism** below with the correct way that it obtains **nitrogen**.

Plants	By breaking down dead organisms and animal waste
Animals	From nitrates in the soil
Bacteria	By eating other organisms

Q3   The nitrogen cycle is dependent on a number of different types of **microorganism**. Explain the role of each of the following types of **bacteria** in the nitrogen cycle.

Type of bacteria   **Role in the nitrogen cycle**

a)   Decomposers   ....

b)   Nitrifying bacteria   ....

c)   Denitrifying bacteria   ....

d)   Nitrogen-fixing bacteria   ....

Q4   Below is a diagram of the **nitrogen cycle**. Explain what is shown by the arrows labelled:

a)   X   ....
....
....

b)   Y   ....
....
....

c)   Z   ....
....
....

Q5   A farmer was told that if he planted **legume plants** his soil would be more **fertile**. Explain how the legume plants would increase the fertility of the soil.

....
....

<u>*Life on Mars*</u>

Q1 From the list below, underline any factors that need to be **balanced** in a **biosphere**.

The amount of carbon dioxide produced and used.   The numbers of plants and animals.

The amount of oxygen produced and used.

Photosynthesis and respiration.   Fuel use and fuel production.

Q2 In the table, tick the columns to show in general which **organisms** carry out these **processes**.

Process	Animals	Plants	Microorganisms
Make food			
Produce oxygen			
Produce carbon dioxide			
Use oxygen			
Use carbon dioxide			

Q3 Read the passage below about an experiment in an **artificial biosphere** in Arizona, Biosphere 2, and then answer the questions which follow.

For two years, biosphere 2 was sealed and monitored so that scientists could see if a safe equilibrium could be established within it. There was a problem with falling oxygen levels, and eventually the scientists had to pump in pure oxygen to keep the biosphere going. The scientists thought that the oxygen had been used up by microorganisms which had been put into the soil to encourage plant growth. However, the carbon dioxide levels would then have increased, but they had not. It was eventually found that concrete in the base of the facility had been absorbing CO_2, and this had reduced plant growth and caused a fall in oxygen levels.

a) What process in the microorganisms would have used up oxygen?

....

b) Why did the scientists expect an increase in CO_2 levels if the microorganisms were responsible?

....

c) How would introducing microorganisms 'encourage plant growth'?

....

....

d) Explain how the absorption of CO_2 by the concrete could have led to a fall in oxygen levels.

....

....

Life on Mars

Q4 Look at the data showing details of the **atmosphere** and **temperature** range on **Earth** and **Mars**.

Planet	% oxygen in atmosphere	% CO₂ in atmosphere	Temperature range (°C)	Average temp. (°C)
Earth	21	0.04	-89.2 – +56.7	+15
Mars	0.13	95.32	-140 – +20	-63

a) From this data, give two factors that would make it hard for organisms from Earth to live on Mars.

....

....

b) One way that humans may be able to survive on Mars would be if they set up an artificial biosphere there. This has already been tried on Earth in **Biosphere 2** in Arizona.

i) Do you think Biosphere 2 was useful for scientists planning a possible settlement on Mars? Give reasons for your answer.

....

....

ii) Explain why it could be difficult to set up a similar biosphere on Mars.

....

....

Q5 Jane set up an experiment to see what effect **plants** and **animals** had on their **environment**. She used aquatic plants and snails, and bicarbonate indicator.

Bicarbonate indicator is red. If carbon dioxide is added, it goes **yellow**. If carbon dioxide is removed, it goes **purple**. Jane set up her experiment as shown in the diagram.

a) Give the colour you would expect the indicator to be after 24 hours in each tube.

A .... B ....

C .... D ....

b) Why did Jane include tube D in her experiment?

....

c) State **two** things that Jane should do in order to make this a fair test.

....

....

There's Too Many People

Q1 Standards of living are **improving** in nearly all countries of the world.
Explain how this is causing **environmental problems**.

....

....

Q2 The size of the Earth's **population** has an impact on our **environment**.

a) Use the table below to plot a graph
on the grid, showing how the world's
human population has changed over
the last 1000 years.

NO. OF PEOPLE (BILLIONS)	YEAR
0.3	1000
0.4	1200
0.4	1400
0.6	1600
1.0	1800
1.7	1900
6.1	2000

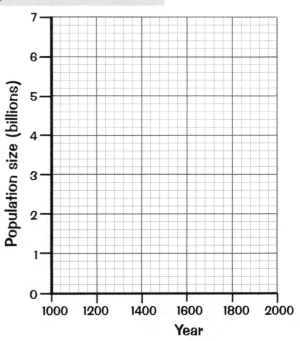

b) Suggest two reasons for the sudden
increase after 1800.

....

....

Q3 The Earth receives energy from the **Sun**. It radiates much of this energy back out to space.

a) Explain the role of the greenhouse gases in keeping the Earth warm.

....

....

b) What would happen if there were no greenhouse gases?

....

c) In recent years the amount of greenhouse gases in the atmosphere has increased.
Explain how this is thought to be leading to global warming.

....

....

There's Too Many People

Q4   Deforestation increases the amount of **carbon dioxide** released into the atmosphere and decreases the amount removed.

a)   Give two reasons why humans cut forests down.

....

....

b)   Give two reasons why deforestation increases the concentration of atmospheric carbon dioxide.

....

....

c)   Give one reason why deforestation reduces the amount of CO_2 removed from the atmosphere.

....

d)   Give two other examples of human activities that release carbon dioxide into the atmosphere.

....

Q5   Global **waste production** has increased as population sizes and living standards have risen. To avoid **polluting** our environment, we need to **recycle** as much of this waste as possible.

The graph shows how the percentage of waste **recycled** in England grew between 1997 and 2004. A line has been drawn on the graph to show the trend in the data.

a)   What percentage of waste was recycled in 2000? ....

b)   If this trend continued, approximately what percentage of waste would be recycled in 2005?

....

c)   State **two** ways that recycling waste helps to conserve the world's energy supplies.

....

....

Climate Change and Food Distribution

Q1 Global warming may cause the seas to warm and **expand**, putting low lying areas at increased risk from **flooding**. This isn't the only possible consequence though — fill in the flow chart to show how temperatures might **decrease**.

Higher temperatures make ice melt.
Ocean currents are disrupted.

Some areas (maybe the UK) get colder.
Cold fresh water enters the ocean.

Q2 One UK newspaper said that **global warming** will be good for the UK because people will be able to have more **barbecues**. Do you think the newspaper is right? Explain your answer.

....

....

Q3 Many countries in the EU have **food surpluses**.

a) How have these food surpluses come about?

....

b) Suggest two problems that might occur if these surpluses were given to countries where there's a food shortage.

....

....

Q4 Southern Sudan, in north Africa, has one of the most severe **food shortages** on Earth. Reasons that have been given for this include the following:

There has been war and conflict for half a century.

Rainfall is low.

Agriculture is very basic.

It's one of the world's poorest countries.

a) How could wars have caused food shortages?

....

b) Suggest what could be done to help with the food shortage in the long term.

....

Food Production

Q1 Three different **food chains** are shown here.

Grass → Cow → Human

Pondweed → Small fish → Salmon → Human

Wheat → Human

a) Circle the food chain that shows the most efficient production of food for humans.

b) Explain your choice.

....

Q2 Emma compared two ecosystems shown in the table. **Ecosystem A** was carefully controlled — the fish were kept in large cages and fed a special diet. Pesticides were used to kill unwanted pests. **Ecosystem B** was kept as natural as possible, with no cages, special diet or pest control.

Time in mths	Number of fish		Average size of fish (mm)		Comments	
	A	B	A	B	A	B
0	200	200	362	348	200 fish introduced.	200 fish introduced.
2	189	191	368	392	A few initial losses due to change in habitat.	A few initial losses due to change in habitat. Initial growth rate seems fast.
4	188	152	374	423	Numbers stabilised. Water quality good.	High numbers of fish lice. Adults still growing well.
6	277	136	436	426	Breeding looks successful. Fish growth increasing.	Fish lice levels still high. Breeding has started. Growth rate decreasing.
8	349	172	359	372	End of breeding season. Adult fish growing well.	Breeding season. Fish numbers stabilising. Water pH 8.
10	338	184	401	382	Very few new fish have been lost.	Breeding season now over. Growth has slowed.
12	336	179	443	393	Population stable. Large, healthy fish.	Population stabilising. Water pH improved at 7.5.

a) Suggest why the average size of the fish drops so much in both ecosystems at 8 months.

....

b) What factors may have affected the growth rate and number of fish in Ecosystem B?

....

c) What conclusions could Emma draw from her investigation?

....

....

Q3 Jim wants to boost the growth of his vegetables, so he builds a **greenhouse**.

a) What is the main reason for the increase in plant growth inside a greenhouse?

....

b) Give two other conditions that can be altered artificially in a greenhouse to increase growth.

1. ....

2. ....

Population Sizes

Q1 Draw lines below to link the **biological terms** on the left with any **examples** on the right.

Adaptation

Competition

Predation

A lion eats an antelope.

Plants of different species in a meadow all need light.

Grasses that grow in dry areas have longer roots.

A bear eats a fish.

Animals in a rock pool all get their oxygen from the water.

Q2 Look at the diagram of a **food web** and answer the questions that follow.

a) Which organism is the whole food web dependent on?
Explain your answer.

....

....

....

b) Name two organisms which you would expect to be competing with each other. Explain your answer.

....

....

....

....

fox

tawny owl

stoat

blue tit

wood mouse

woodpecker

squirrel

caterpillar

spider

ladybird

greenfly

oak tree

c) Suggest what might happen to the population of the spiders if pesticides killed off most of the greenfly. Give a reason for your answer.

....

....

Q3 **Hawks** are large **predators** found at the tops of their food webs.
A hawk is shown in the diagram.

Give three ways that a hawk is adapted to being a carnivore.

....

....

....

....

Eyes at front of head allow good judgment of distance

Sharp beak with hooked end

Large, strong wings

Sharp claws

Thick layers of feathers provide insulation

Population Sizes

Q4 It is common for the males of many species to set up **territories** (areas where they are the only male). They will fight off any other males that try to enter their territory.

Suggest why having a territory is a useful adaptation.

....

....

Q5 **Herring** and **cod** are fish that are caught for food in the North Sea. The graph shows the size of the fish populations (measured in biomass) over the last thirty years. Herring fishing in the North Sea was **banned** between 1978 and 1982.

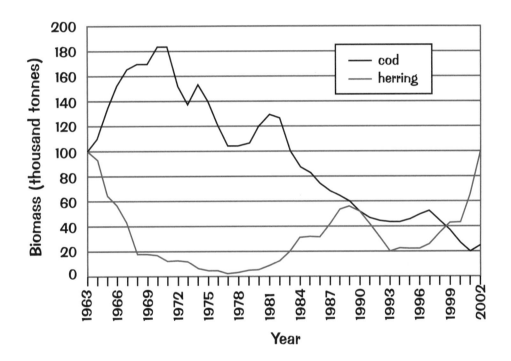

a) Between what years was the **cod** population at its highest level? ....

b) Describe the changes seen in the number of **herring** in the North Sea between 1963 and 1989.

....

....

c) Suggest an explanation for the changes you described above.

....

....

d) Use this data to suggest **one** thing that could be done to help the cod population survive.

....

Extreme Environments

Q1   The picture below shows an **angler fish**. Angler fish live
in very **deep seas**, where sunlight cannot penetrate.

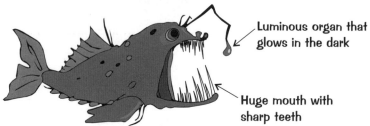

Luminous organ that
glows in the dark

Huge mouth with
sharp teeth

a)   What conditions make the deep sea a hostile environment?

....

....

b)   Suggest how the following features help the angler fish to stay alive in its environment:

i)   The luminous organ on its head.

....

ii) Its huge mouth.

....

Q2   There is usually a much higher density of life found on the seabed around **hot vents**.

a)   Give two things that are provided by the hot vents that make it easier for life to exist around them.

....

b)   The food webs around hot vents are not based on photosynthesis, unlike most others on Earth.

i)   Name the process that hot vent food webs rely on.

....

ii) Briefly explain how this process works.

....

....

c)   Name the type of organism found at the bottom of hot
vent food webs.

....

Extreme Environments

Q3 List three difficulties that organisms living at **high altitude** face.

1. ....

2. ....

3. ....

Q4 When a major **sports event** is held in a country that is at a **high altitude**, the participants usually go out to the country some time before the event in order to 'acclimatise' to the lower levels of **oxygen**. The graph below shows how their **fitness** changes after arrival at high altitude.

a) Describe the change in fitness shown by the graph.

....

....

b) Suggest how a lack of oxygen might lead to a drop in performance at a sports event.

....

....

c) Athletes that have acclimatised have more red blood cells. How will this help them to perform?

....

Q5 Penguins living in the **Antarctic** have to survive very low temperatures. They have feathers, which trap air to form an **insulating layer**, and a thick layer of **fat** under their skin. The only places on their bodies that do not have a thick insulating layer are the feet and the flippers.

a) The muscles that operate a penguin's feet and flippers are not actually in these parts of its body, but in the main part of the body. Explain why this is important.

....

....

b) The penguin needs these muscles to propel it through the water. Suggest why many of the animals found in the Antarctic are adapted for swimming.

....

....

Top Tip: **Extreme environments** are places with conditions that few species can cope with. For those that can, life's no picnic but on the plus side there's **very little competition** from other species.

Air Pollution — CO_2 and CO

Q1 **Exhaust fumes** from cars and lorries often contain **carbon monoxide**.

a) Why is this more likely to be formed in engines than if the fuel was burnt in the open air?

....

....

b) Why is carbon monoxide so dangerous?

....

Q2 Look at the graph and then answer the questions below.

a) Describe the **trend** shown by the graph.

....

....

....

....

b) What is the main cause of this trend?

....

c) What effect do many scientists believe the trend shown in the graph is having on the Earth's average temperature?

....

Q3 The maps show the results of a study into **carbon monoxide pollution** in an area of England.

Towns and villages in study area (in dark grey) with road connections.

Pollution by carbon monoxide: dark blue = high, pale blue = medium, white = low.

a) Describe and explain the pattern of pollution shown on the maps.

....

....

b) What evidence is there that motor vehicles are a major source of carbon monoxide pollution?

....

Interpreting Data: Climate Change

Q1 Two university students carried out **observations**. Student A noticed that a glacier was melting. Student B noticed that daffodils flowered earlier in 2006 than in 2005. Both students concluded that this was due to **global warming**. Are they right? Explain your answer.

....

....

Q2 Scientists are collecting **evidence** to try to support or disprove the **theory** of global warming.

Give examples of the sort of data that scientists are collecting about climate change.

....

....

Q3 Many scientists think that the Earth is **warming up**. The graph shows the mean temperature between **1961** and **1990**, and how the temperature has differed from it over the last **300 years**.

a) Does this graph support the theory that the Earth is getting warmer? Explain your answer.

....

....

b) What do some scientists think is responsible for this increase in temperature?

....

....

In order to study possible global warming, scientists have looked at the Earth's temperature over a very long period. The graph on the left shows the temperature variations over the last 2000 years (older temperatures are worked out by studying the effects they had on bodies of water, glaciers and living things).

c) Some scientists believe that the current temperature rise is the result of normal long-term temperature variation. Look at the graph and explain whether or not it supports this idea.

....

....

Air Pollution — Acid Rain

Q1   Draw lines to match each sentence with the best ending.

The main cause of acid rain is

Acid rain kills trees and

Limestone buildings and statues are affected by

In clouds sulphur dioxide reacts with water to make

acid rain.

sulphuric acid.

acidifies lakes.

sulphur dioxide.

Q2   Use the words and phrases below to complete the paragraph.

nitric	sulphur dioxide	carbon dioxide	sulphuric	nitrogen oxides	acid rain

When fossil fuels are burned, ... is produced. This causes the greenhouse

effect. The gas .... is also produced. This comes from sulphur impurities

in the fuel. When it combines with moisture in the air .... acid is produced

and falls as acid rain. In the high temperature inside a car engine, nitrogen and oxygen from the

air react together to produce .... These react with moisture to produce

.... acid, which is another cause of acid rain.

Q3   Ben was investigating the effect of **acid rain** on the **germination** of cress seeds. He set up six sets of apparatus (as shown in the diagram), five with a different **strength of acid** in the container and one with water only. He left them for three days and then calculated the percentage of seeds that had germinated. His results are shown on the graph.

a)   Estimate the percentage germination
        if Ben had used 0.4 M acid.   ....

b)   What conclusions could Ben draw from his experiment?

....

....

....

c)   Why did Ben set up an experiment with just water and no acid?

....

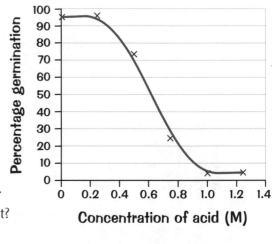

Water Pollution

Q1 Suggest one way that each of the following **pollutants** can get into rivers and streams.

a) Pesticides.

....

b) Oil.

....

c) Metals.

....

Q2 This is a **food chain** based around a stream.

Algae → Water louse → Dragonfly nymph → Water shrew → Kestrel

a) If the stream is polluted by a pesticide such as DDT, which of the organisms in the food chain is most likely to suffer?

....

b) Explain your answer to part **a)**.

....

....

Q3 Scientists tested the water in a river before and after it passed a farm. The farm was suspected of polluting the river with **sewage**. Direct measurements of the levels of **nitrogen**, **phosphorus** and **oxygen** were taken. Complete the table below by ticking the appropriate boxes to show how you would expect the water to be different after passing the farm if it was polluting the river.

Chemical	Level rises	Level stays the same	Level falls
Nitrogen			
Phosphorus			
Oxygen			

Water Pollution

Q4 Environment officers monitored two **polluted rivers**. One had been polluted with **fertiliser**, the other with a **heavy metal poison**. Numbers of two insect species were counted in the rivers — **rat-tailed maggots**, which survive well in oxygen-depleted water, and **stonefly larvae**, which need a high level of oxygen.

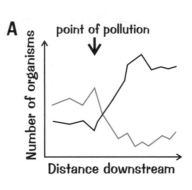

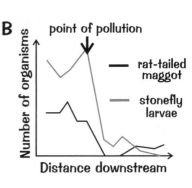

a) Complete the following: The river polluted with **fertiliser** is shown on graph ....

The river polluted with a **heavy metal** is shown on graph ....

b) Explain the differences seen in the graphs for the two rivers.

....

....

....

Q5 The graph shows the numbers of serious incidents of **water pollution** in different areas of a European country between 2002-2005.

a) Which area had the least pollution incidents

   i) in 2002? ....

   ii) in 2003? ....

b) Does the graph give evidence for a fall in water pollution between 2004 and 2005? Explain your answer.

   ....

   ....

   ....

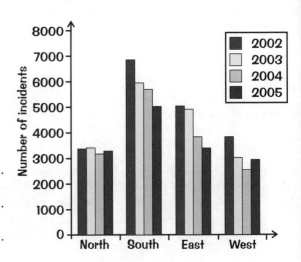

c) Suggest a reason why there are many more pollution incidents in the South of this country than in the West.

....

....

Top Tip: A **direct measurement** of water pollution is made by testing a sample to check the levels of different chemicals. An **indirect measurement** is made by looking at what's living in the water.

Living Indicators

Q1 **Mayfly larvae** and **sludge worms** are often studied to see how much **sewage** is in water.

a) What is the name for an organism used in this way?

....

Juanita recorded the number of each species in water samples taken at three different distances downstream from a sewage outlet. Her results are shown below.

Distance (m)	No. of mayfly larvae	No. of sludge worms
20	3	20
40	11	14
60	23	7

b) State **one** thing that she would have to do to make this experiment a fair test.

....

c) What can you conclude about the two organisms from these results?

....

....

....

Q2 Tick the right boxes to say whether the sentences below are **true** or **false**.

		True	False
a)	All pollution comes from factories and power stations.	☐	☐
b)	Lichens can be used as indicator species for air pollution.	☐	☐
c)	Lichens prefer areas of low air quality.	☐	☐
d)	The number of cases of skin cancer is also an indicator of pollution.	☐	☐
e)	Skin cancer is caused by high levels of sulphur dioxide in the atmosphere.	☐	☐
f)	Damage to the ozone layer means it absorbs more radiation from the Sun.	☐	☐

Q3 Underline any substance known to damage the **ozone layer**.

Methane   Carbon dioxide

CFCs   Sulphur dioxide

Living Indicators

Q4 Use the words in the box to complete the following passage about the thinning **ozone layer**.

infra-red	aerosols	oxygen	CFCs	cars	ozone
ultraviolet	skin cancer	nitrous oxides	lung cancer		

The Earth's atmosphere has a layer of .... in it. This layer protects

the planet from .... radiation. Over the last thirty years there has

been a thinning of the layer due to air pollution by ...., which are

gases used in ...., air conditioning and refrigerator coolants.

The thinning of this layer is a concern because the radiation that gets through

can cause ....

Q5 The number of species of **lichen** living in an area can be used as an **indicator** of how **clean** the air is there. Scientists did a survey of the number of lichens found on gravestones at different distances from a city centre. The results are shown below:

Distance from city centre (km)	No. of species found on ten gravestones
0	12
2	13
6	22
16	29
20	15
24	35

No. of species of lichen

Distance from city centre (km)

a) Draw a graph of this data on the grid provided.

b) State two precautions that the scientists would have needed to take when doing the experiment in order to ensure that the test was fair.

....

....

c) What **general trend** is shown by the data?

....

....

d) The result at 20 km is **anomalous** — it doesn't fit the general trend. Suggest a possible reason for this.

....

Conservation

Q1   One of the aims of **conservation** is to maintain the **biodiversity** in a habitat.

Explain what is meant by **biodiversity**, and why is it important to preserve biodiversity in a habitat.

....

....

Q2   The stocks of **cod** in the waters around Britain have greatly decreased. Most of the fish caught are about two years old. Cod mature and start to **reproduce** at about 4–5 years old. It has been suggested that using nets with a **larger mesh size** might help to conserve the stocks.

  a)   Why would it be better if fish were caught **after** they had reached their reproductive age?

....

  b)   Why might increasing the **mesh size** of fishing nets help to conserve stocks?

....

  c)   Give one reason why it is important to preserve the stocks of cod in the waters around Britain.

....

Q3   Suggest **three** methods that can be used to conserve **woodland**.

....

....

Q4   The **elephant population** in an African national park (a conservation area) is growing rapidly. Large numbers of elephants **damage** their habitat, trampling plants that other animals need for food. During the last century, the elephants were '**culled**' for a time (the 'extra' elephants were shot). The growth of the elephant population is shown in the graph.

  a)   From the graph, suggest when the 'cull' started and ended.

....

  b)   The national park was set up in 1905.
Suggest why the elephant population was so low at the time.

....

  c)   Suggest **one** alternative way of reducing the elephant population without 'culling'.

....

<u>*Recycling*</u>

Q1 Tick the boxes to show which of the following are good reasons for **recycling metals**.

☐ The recycling process gives many metals useful new properties.

☐ It uses less energy and therefore less fossil fuel.

☐ The metal produced is purer and so of a higher quality.

☐ Less carbon dioxide is produced as a result.

Q2 Most plastics are **not** biodegradable.

Biodegradable means that something can rot.

a) What problems does this cause for the environment?

....

....

b) How can you minimise this environmental problem when using objects made from plastics?

....

c) Things are often made from plastics because they are cheap. Why might this change in the future?

....

....

Q3 There are important **benefits** of recycling, but it is still **not** a perfect solution.

a) Explain how recycling materials helps to conserve the world's energy resources.

....

....

b) State three ways in which the recycling process uses energy.

1. ....

2. ....

3. ....

Recycling

Q4 The diagram shows the changes in the amounts of different materials **recycled** through **kerbside collection schemes** from 2002–2004.

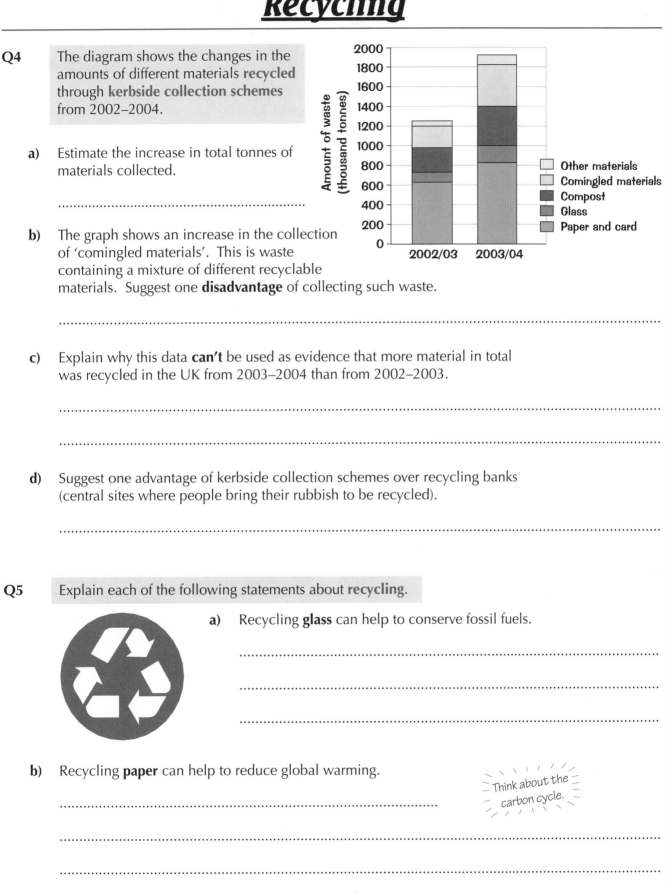

a) Estimate the increase in total tonnes of materials collected.

....

b) The graph shows an increase in the collection of 'comingled materials'. This is waste containing a mixture of different recyclable materials. Suggest one **disadvantage** of collecting such waste.

....

c) Explain why this data **can't** be used as evidence that more material in total was recycled in the UK from 2003–2004 than from 2002–2003.

....

....

d) Suggest one advantage of kerbside collection schemes over recycling banks (central sites where people bring their rubbish to be recycled).

....

Q5 Explain each of the following statements about **recycling**.

a) Recycling **glass** can help to conserve fossil fuels.

....

....

....

b) Recycling **paper** can help to reduce global warming.

Think about the carbon cycle.

....

....

....

Top Tip: The UK isn't too great at recycling — we're getting better, but still languishing far behind other European countries. Collection schemes are making things easier, so no more excuses.

Mixed Questions — B2 Topics 3 & 4

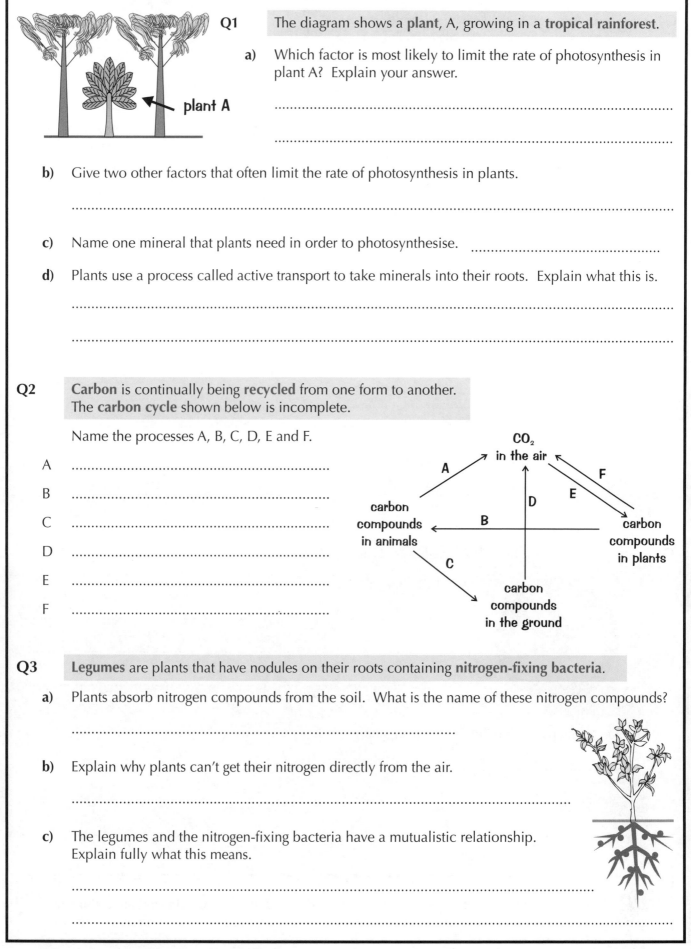

Q1 The diagram shows a **plant**, A, growing in a **tropical rainforest**.

a) Which factor is most likely to limit the rate of photosynthesis in plant A? Explain your answer.

....

....

b) Give two other factors that often limit the rate of photosynthesis in plants.

....

c) Name one mineral that plants need in order to photosynthesise. ....

d) Plants use a process called active transport to take minerals into their roots. Explain what this is.

....

....

Q2 **Carbon** is continually being **recycled** from one form to another. The **carbon cycle** shown below is incomplete.

Name the processes A, B, C, D, E and F.

A ....

B ....

C ....

D ....

E ....

F ....

Q3 **Legumes** are plants that have nodules on their roots containing **nitrogen-fixing bacteria**.

a) Plants absorb nitrogen compounds from the soil. What is the name of these nitrogen compounds?

....

b) Explain why plants can't get their nitrogen directly from the air.

....

c) The legumes and the nitrogen-fixing bacteria have a mutualistic relationship. Explain fully what this means.

....

....

Mixed Questions — B2 Topics 3 & 4

Q4 The Earth's **human population** has been **increasing** more and more rapidly for many years.

a) Explain how the growing population is thought to be altering the Earth's **climate**.

....

....

....

....

b) It has been suggested that if the Earth's population increases to a completely unsustainable level, it might be possible to colonise Mars.

i) Explain why the natural environment on Mars could not support life.

....

ii) How could life from Earth survive on Mars?

....

Q5 The graph shows how the **populations** of **snowy owls** and **lemmings** in a community vary over time.

Describe and explain the reasons for the population trends shown on the graph.

....

....

....

....

Q6 The picture shows an animal that is **adapted** to survive in an **extreme environment**. Its fur is white and it is a carnivore.

a) Suggest the type of habitat where you would expect to find this animal.

....

b) Give three features that the animal has evolved to cope in this climate and briefly explain how each feature helps the animal to survive.

....

....

....

B2 Topic 4 — Interdependence

Mixed Questions — B2 Topics 3 & 4

Q7 Human activity causes various types of **air pollution**. Four common air pollutants are:

$$CO_2 \qquad CO \qquad SO_2 \qquad NO_x$$

Each statement below refers to one or more of these pollutants. Indicate which one(s) in the space provided.

a) May be released when fossil fuels are burnt. ......CO_2...

b) Amount in the atmosphere is increased by deforestation. ....CO_2......................................

c) Linked with global warming and climate change. .....CO_2..

d) A poisonous gas that prevents red blood cells carrying oxygen. ...NO_x..............................

e) Cause acid rain when they mix with clouds. .....SO_2...

f) Comes from impurities in fossil fuels. ...NO_x..

Q8 **Water pollution** can be measured both **directly** and **indirectly**.

a) Explain what each of these methods involves.

....

....

b) A sample of water is taken from two different streams. The sample from stream A contains 19 organisms of two different species. The sample from stream B contain 36 organisms of eight different species. Which stream do you think is the more polluted? Explain your answer.

....

....

Q9 Woodland Industries is a company that produces **wood** for **manufacturing paper**. They have introduced several measures to ensure that the woodland habitats used are **conserved**.

a) Explain what each of the following measures involves:

i) Reforestation ....

ii) Coppicing ....

iii) Replacement planting ....

b) These measures allow Woodland Industries to produce a constant supply of paper without losing the woodland habitat. Explain why it would still be worthwhile to recycle the paper they make.

....

....

c) - One of the English woods owned by Woodland Industries contains several old oak trees. The company has agreed with the local council not to fell the trees because they are part of England's 'cultural heritage'. Explain what this means.

....

Balancing Equations

Q1 Three boys were asked to balance the equation for making **water** for their homework.
Tick one box to show which of them got it right.

Rio:	H_2	+	O_2	$\rightarrow$	H_2O_2	☑
Stevie:	$2H_2$	+	O_2	$\rightarrow$	$2H_2O$	☐
Wayne:	H_2	+	O_2	$\rightarrow$	$2H_2O$	☐

Q2 **Methane** (CH_4) burns in **oxygen** to make **water** and **carbon dioxide**.

a) Write the balanced symbol equation for this reaction.

....

b) If the amount of oxygen available is limited, the products of the reaction are carbon monoxide
and water. Write the balanced symbol equation for this reaction.

....

Q3 **Balance** each of the following equations.

a) $FeCl_2$ + Cl_2 $\rightarrow$ $FeCl_3$

....

b) Al + Cl_2 $\rightarrow$ $AlCl_3$

....

c) N_2 + H_2 $\rightarrow$ NH_3

....

Q4 **Eicosane** ($C_{20}H_{42}$) is a type of wax. It burns in oxygen to make water and carbon dioxide.
Write a balanced equation for the combustion of eicosane.

....

Q5 **Ammonia** (NH_3) can be converted into **nitric acid** by a series of reactions involving oxygen.
The first step can be represented by this equation, which is currently unbalanced. **Balance it**.

NH_3 + O_2 $\rightarrow$ NO + H_2O

....

Crude Oil

Q1   Which of these substances is **not** made from **crude oil**? Underline your answer.

   plastics   solvents   metals   medicines   detergents

Q2   As crude oil is a **non-renewable** resource, people are keen to find **alternative** energy sources.
Suggest a problem with each of these ways of using alternative fuels.

   a)   **Solar** energy for cars: ....

   ....

   b)   **Wind** energy to power an oven: ....

   ....

   c)   **Nuclear** energy for buses: ....

   ....

Q3   Forty years ago some scientists predicted that there would be no oil left by the year 2000, but
obviously they were **wrong**. One reason is that modern engines are more **efficient** than in the
past, so they use less fuel. Give two other reasons why the scientists' prediction was wrong.

   1. ....

   2. ....

Q4   Carbon is essential for life.

   a)   How many covalent bonds can a carbon atom form?

   ....

   b)   Explain how carbon allows complicated life forms like animals to exist.

   ....

   ....

   ....

Q5   Write a short paragraph summarising why crude oil is the most
common source of fuel even though **alternatives** are available.

   ....

   ....

   ....

Alkanes and Alkenes

Q1 Complete this table showing the **molecular** and **displayed** formulae of some alkenes.

Alkene	Formula	Displayed formula
Ethene	a)	b)
c) Propane	C_3H_6	d)

Q2 The general formula for **alkanes** is C_nH_{2n+2}. Use this to write down the formulae of these alkanes.

a) pentane (5 carbons) ....

b) hexane (6 carbons) ....

c) octane (8 carbons) ....

d) dodecane (12 carbons) ....

Q3 Tick the boxes to show whether the following statements are **true** or **false**.

	True	False

a) Alkenes have double bonds between the hydrogen atoms. ☐ ☐

b) Alkenes are unsaturated. ☐ ☐

c) Alkenes can't form polymers as they have no spare bonds. ☐ ☐

d) Ethene has two carbon atoms. ☐ ☐

No, there's no spare 007s here.

Q4 Both **hexane** and **hexene** are colourless liquids.
Describe a test you could use to tell them apart.

....

....

Q5 The diagram shows a molecule that can be made from **ethene**.

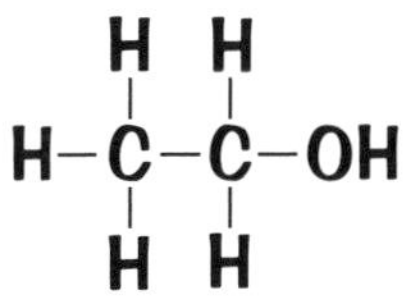

```
    H  H
    |  |
H - C - C - OH
    |  |
    H  H
```

a) Name this molecule. ....

b) Which group of compounds does it belong to? ....

c) Describe how it is made industrially from ethene.

....

....

d) What name is given to this type of process? ....

Cracking Hydrocarbons

Q1   Fill in the gaps by choosing from the words in the box.

high	shorter	long	saturated	catalyst	cracking	diesel
		molecules	petrol	double bond		

There is more need for ...... _shorter_ ...... chain fractions of crude oil such as ...... _petrol_ ......

than for longer chains such as ...... _diesel_ .... Heating ...... _long_ ...... hydrocarbon

molecules to ...... _high_ ...... temperatures with a ...... _catalyst_ ...... breaks them down

into smaller ...... _molecules_ .... This is called ...... _cracking_ ....

Q2   Diesel is **cracked** to produce products that are more in demand.

  a)   Name two useful substances that can be produced when diesel is cracked.

....

  b)   What type of reaction is cracking? ....

Q3   This apparatus can be used to crack a **liquid hydrocarbon** such as **paraffin**.

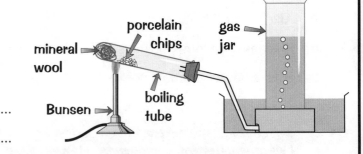

  a)   Where would the paraffin be?

....

....

  b)   What are the porcelain chips for? ....

  c)   What collects at the cooler end of the boiling tube? ....

  d)   What collects in the gas jar? ....

Q4   Change this diagram into a **word equation** and a **symbol equation**.

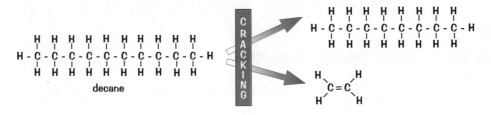

  a)   Word equation: ....   →   ....   + ...

  b)   Symbol equation: ....   →   ....   + ...

Vegetable Oils

Q1   Each diagram shows part of a fat structure. Draw lines to match each label to its correct structure.

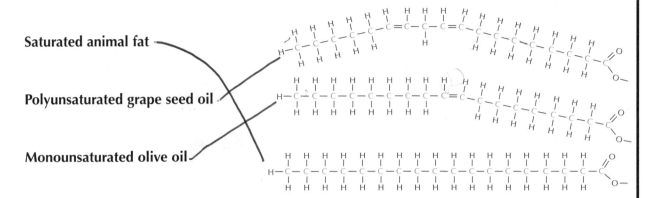

Saturated animal fat

Polyunsaturated grape seed oil

Monounsaturated olive oil

Q2   **Cholesterol** is a substance made in the liver. **Oils** are often classed as healthy or not according to their effect on the amount of cholesterol in the blood.

a)   Give a type of illness which is associated with high levels of cholesterol in the blood.

.....Chronic heart disease.....

b)   Put these types of oil in order of 'healthiness', with the most healthy first.

saturated   polyunsaturated   monounsaturated

..polyunsaturated.......   ...monounsaturated......   ...Saturated.............

c)   Explain what is meant by the terms **saturated** and **unsaturated**.

....

d)   What is the difference between polyunsaturated and monounsaturated molecules?

..polyunsaturated molecules means that there is more than one double bond......
..between a carbon and monounsaturated means that there is just one.....
..double bond.

e)   What process is used to convert polyunsaturated oils into saturated fats?

...Cracking.....

Q3   **Margarine** is usually made from **partially hydrogenated** vegetable oil.

a)   Describe the process of hydrogenation.

...Hydrogenation means adding Hydrogen to an element.........................

....

b)   How does hydrogenation affect the melting points of vegetable oils?

...Increasing the melting points.....

Vegetable Oils

Q4   Complete the passage below using words from the list.

single strong inflexible viscous flexible double can weak straight can't

Saturated oils contain long chains of carbon atoms joined by ....*Single*.......... bonds. This makes them ....~~weak~~ *Strong*.... and ....*inflexible*.........., so they ....*can*.............. pack tightly together. The forces between these molecules are ....~~weak~~ *Strong*.... and so the oils are more ....*Viscous*..........

Q5   Circle the correct word from each pair.

Unsaturated oils have **double** / ~~triple~~ bonds between some of the carbon atoms. These make the molecule ~~kinked~~ / **straight** and ~~flexible~~ / **inflexible** and so they **can** / **can't** pack tightly together. The forces between these molecules are **strong** / **weak** and so the oils are **less** / **more** viscous.

Q6   Many people eat **margarine** and **low-fat spreads** (which are basically margarine and water) as a healthier alternative to butter. Below is part of the **nutritional information** on a packet of butter, a tub of margarine and a tub of low-fat spread. All values are per 100 g.

	BUTTER	MARGARINE	LOW-FAT SPREAD
ENERGY (kJ)	3031	2198	1396
SATURATED FAT (g)	54	19.5	8.7
MONOUNSATURATED FAT (g)	19.8	25.4	17.6
POLYUNSATURATED FAT (g)	2.6	11.4	7.0

saturated fat

a)   Calculate the total amount of fat per 100 g of each product.

....

....

b)   Calculate the percentage of the total fat in each product that is saturated.

....

....

c)   What is the connection between the total amount of fat and the energy supplied by these products?

....

Top Tips: You need to make sure you know the differences between **saturated** and **unsaturated** oils. Then there's the **mono** and **poly**unsaturates. But it's less tricky than it sounds — learn about their properties and their effects on your health, and you'll soon be **saturated** with knowledge. Boom boom.

Plastics

Q1   Tick the box next to the **true** statement below.

☐ The monomer of poly(ethene) is ethene.

☐ The polymer of poly(ethene) is ethane.

☐ The monomer of poly(ethene) is ethane.

We bring you Gold, Frankincense...
and poly-myrrh

Q2   **Addition polymers** are formed when **unsaturated monomers** link together. Special conditions are needed to make this happen.

a)   What feature of the monomer molecules makes them 'unsaturated'?

....

b)   Name two of the 'special conditions' that are used in this reaction.

1. ....

2. ....

Q3   The diagram below shows the polymerisation of ethene to form **poly(ethene)**.

a)   Draw a similar diagram in the box below to show the polymerisation of **propene** (C_3H_6).

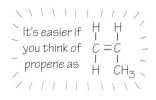

It's easier if you think of propene as

b)   Name the polymer you have drawn. ....

C2 Topic 5 — Synthesis

62

Plastics

Q4 The diagram shows part of the chain of a **polyvinyl chloride** (**PVC**) molecule.

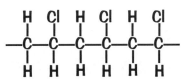

a) Which of these formulae represents the monomer used to make PVC? Tick one box.

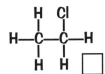   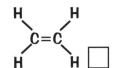

b) Write a displayed equation to show the formation of PVC.

....

c) The diagram below shows part of the chain of a polyphenylethene (polystyrene) molecule. Draw the monomer used to make this polymer in the space provided.

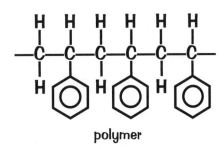

polymer

monomer

Q5 From the list below underline any **properties** you think it is important for a plastic to have if it is to be used to make **Wellington boots**.

low melting point   waterproof   rigid   lightweight   heat resistant

Q6 Most plastics are not readily **biodegradable**.

a) Lots of plastic is buried in landfill sites. Suggest one problem with this method of disposal.

....

b) Another disposal method is to burn the waste plastic. Why might there be a problem with the gases produced?

....

c) Recycling plastics avoids the problems of disposal. What is the main problem with this solution?

....

Plastics

Q7 When old houses are modernised, the **wooden window frames** are often replaced with new ones made from **PVC**.

a) Describe the physical properties of pure PVC.

....

b) Explain why preservatives are added to the PVC used to make window frames.

....

....

Q8 Two rulers, made from **different plastics**, were investigated by bending and heating them. The results are shown in the table.

	RESULT ON BENDING	RESULT ON HEATING
Ruler 1	Ruler bends easily and springs back into shape	Ruler becomes soft and then melts
Ruler 2	Ruler snaps in two	Ruler doesn't soften and eventually turns black

a) Which ruler is made from a polymer that has **strong** forces between its molecules? ....

b) The atoms in both types of plastic are held together with the same strong covalent bonds. Explain why one type of plastic melts and bends more easily than the other.

....

....

Q9 Two types of **polythene** are manufactured from ethene using different reaction conditions. One is **high density polythene** (HDP) and the other is **low density polythene** (LDP).

The table compares some of their properties.

	DENSITY	SOFTENING TEMP.	FLEXIBILITY
LDP	Low	Below 100 °C	High
HDP	High	Above 100 °C	Fairly low

For each of the following applications choose which type of polythene should be used and give a reason for your choice.

a) toothpaste tubes ....

....

b) freezer bags ....

....

c) drain pipes ....

....

d) hospital equipment that has to be sterilised ....

....

Plastics

Q10 **Polymer** molecules are **long chains**, as shown in the diagrams.

A

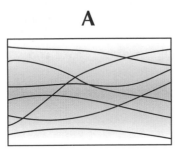

B

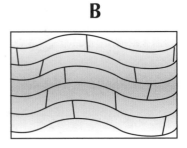

Which diagram shows a **thermosetting** polymer? Explain your answer.

....

....

Q11 Some carrier bags are made from **recycled polythene**.

a) What is the raw material used to make plastics?

....

b) Use what you know **about this raw material** to explain why it is a good idea to recycle plastics.

....

....

c) Describe three types of degradable plastic which have been developed recently.

....

....

....

....

....

d) Newly developed plastics have to be tested to see exactly
what is produced when they break down. Explain why.

....

Top Tips: Plastics are really useful materials, and completely **man-made**. Well done us.
But there aren't any organisms that can **break them down**, and they're also made out of **crude oil**,
which is a bit of a shame. Maybe not quite so well done us.

Drug Synthesis

Q1 Read the passage below and answer the questions that follow.

> In 1763 a scientific paper was written describing the success of an extract of willow bark in treating fevers (high temperatures). It was later discovered that the bark contained a substance called salicylic acid, and for a hundred years this was used to treat fevers and rheumatism. Unfortunately, it was unpleasant to take and caused stomach and mouth ulcers. Because of this, many people couldn't take it.
>
> In 1899 a substance called aspirin was first marketed. A known reaction — esterification — was used to modify the structure of salicylic acid. Aspirin had the useful properties of salicylic acid but fewer of the unpleasant side effects.

a) What unwanted side effects did salicylic acid have?

....

b) Give one way that aspirin can be produced.

....

c) Why do you think that this method of producing aspirin was tried?

....

d) What were the benefits of the new drug, aspirin?

....

Q2 It's not just guess-work when chemists are creating new chemicals.

a) Why do chemists use information about known reactions when making new drugs?

....

....

b) Why is this method of drug synthesis better than if chemists guessed when creating chemicals.

....

....

c) What are the difficulties faced when creating and marketing new drugs?

....

....

Drug Synthesis

Q3 Before use, drugs go through a long process of **testing**.
Put the steps below in order to show the correct sequence of such tests.

A Large groups of patients are tested, with some of them being given a placebo.

B The drug is tested on cultures of living cells and on animals.

C Healthy human volunteers are given the drug in slowly increasing amounts.

D Small groups of people with the disease are tested.

Order: ....

Q4 Most modern drugs are made by a process called **staged synthesis**.

a) Describe how a drug **ABC** could be made by staged synthesis from compounds A, B and C.

....

....

b) How would a drug company make a 'family' of new drugs similar to ABC?

....

....

Q5 A drug company wants to make a **family** of compounds similar to a successful new drug, **PQR**.
They have 2 **P-type** compounds (P1 and P2), 2 **Q-type** compounds (Q1 and Q2) and 2 **R-type** compounds (R1 and R2).

a) List the possible combinations to show how they could make eight new compounds.

....

....

b) Calculate how many compounds the company could make if they had 15 of each type.

....

....

Relative Formula Mass

Q1 a) What is meant by the **relative atomic mass** of an element?

It is the number of proton and neutrons in an element.

b) What are the **relative atomic masses (A_r)** of the following:

i)	magnesium	24	**iv)**	hydrogen	1	**vii)** K	39

i) magnesium _24_   **iv)** hydrogen _1_   **vii)** K _39_

ii) neon _20_   **v)** C _12_   **viii)** Ca _40_

iii) oxygen _16_   **vi)** Cu _63.5_   **ix)** Cl _35.5_

Q2 **Identify** the **elements** A, B and C.

Element A is _Helium_

Element B is _Carbon_

Element C is _Oxygen_

> Element A has an A_r of 4.
> Element B has an A_r 3 times that of element A.
> Element C has an A_r 4 times that of element A.

Q3 a) Explain how the **relative formula mass** of a **compound** is calculated.

This is the Sum of the relative atomic masses of all its elements added together

b) What are the **relative formula masses (M_r)** of the following:

i) water (H_2O) _18_

ii) potassium hydroxide (KOH) _56_

iii) nitric acid (HNO_3) _63_

iv) sulphuric acid (H_2SO_4) _96_

v) ammonium nitrate (NH_4NO_3) _80_

vi) aluminium sulphate ($Al_2(SO_4)_3$) _293_

Q4 The equation below shows a reaction between an element, X, and water. The total M_r of the products is **114**. What is substance X?

$$2X + 2H_2O \rightarrow 2XOH + H_2$$

Potassium

Top Tips: The **periodic table** really comes in useful here. There's no way you'll be able to answer these questions without one (unless you've memorised all the elements' relative atomic masses — and that would just be **silly**). And luckily for you, there's one in the front of this book.

68

Empirical Formulae

Q1 What is the **empirical formula** of each of these substances?

a) H_2O_2 ....HO........

b) H_2O ....H_2O........

c) C_2H_4 ....CH_2........

d) C_4H_8 ....CH_2........

e) CH_3COOH ....CHOOH........

Q2 A hydrocarbon contains 6 g of **carbon** and 2 g of **hydrogen**. Calculate its **empirical formula**.

....

....

....

Q3 1.48 g of a **calcium compound** contains 0.8 g calcium, 0.64 g oxygen and 0.04 g hydrogen.

Work out the empirical formula of the compound.

....

....

....

Q4 16 g of **copper** makes 20 g of **copper oxide**. Calculate the **empirical formula** of copper oxide.

....

....

....

Q5 A sugar found in honey contains **40% carbon**, **6.67% hydrogen** and **53.33% oxygen**.

a) Calculate its empirical formula.

....

....

....

b) The molecular mass of the sugar is 180. What is its molecular formula?

....

....

<u>Calculating Masses in Reactions</u>

Q1 Anna burns **10 g** of **magnesium** in air to produce **magnesium oxide** (MgO).

   a) Write out the **balanced equation** for this reaction.

....

   b) Calculate the mass of **magnesium oxide** that's produced.

....

....

....

Q2 What mass of **sodium** is needed to make **2 g** of **sodium oxide**? $4Na + O_2 \rightarrow 2Na_2O$

....

....

....

Q3 **Aluminium** and **iron oxide** (Fe_2O_3) react together to produce **aluminium oxide** (Al_2O_3) and **iron**.

   a) Write out the **balanced equation** for this reaction.

....

   b) What **mass** of iron is produced from **20 g** of iron oxide?

....

....

....

Q4 When heated, **limestone** ($CaCO_3$) decomposes to form **calcium oxide** (CaO) and **carbon dioxide**.

How many **kilograms** of limestone are needed to make **100 kilograms** of **calcium oxide**?

The calculation is the same — just use 'kg' instead of 'g'.

....

....

....

....

Calculating Masses in Reactions

Q5 Iron oxide is reduced to **iron** inside a blast furnace using carbon. There are **three** stages involved.

Stage A $C + O_2 \rightarrow CO_2$

Stage B $CO_2 + C \rightarrow 2CO$

Stage C $3CO + Fe_2O_3 \rightarrow 2Fe + 3CO_2$

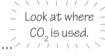

a) If **10 g** of **carbon** are used in stage B, and all the carbon monoxide produced gets used in stage C, what **mass** of CO_2 is produced in **stage C**?

.... *Work out the mass*
of CO at the end of
.... *stage B first.*

....

....

b) Suggest what happens to the CO_2 produced in stage C.   *Look at where*
CO_2 is used.

....

Q6 **Sodium sulphate** (Na_2SO_4) is made by reacting **sodium hydroxide** (NaOH) with **sulphuric acid** (H_2SO_4). **Water** is also produced.

a) Write out the **balanced equation** for this reaction.

....

b) What mass of **sodium hydroxide** is needed to make **75 g** of **sodium sulphate**?

....

....

....

....

c) What mass of **water** is formed when **50 g** of **sulphuric acid** reacts with sodium sulphate?

....

....

....

....

Top Tips: Masses, equations, formulae — they can all seem a bit scary. But don't worry, practice makes perfect. And once you get the hang of them you'll wonder what all the fuss was about.

Atom Economy

Q1 **Copper oxide** can be reduced to copper by heating it with carbon.

> copper oxide + carbon → copper + carbon dioxide
>
> $2CuO + C \rightarrow 2Cu + CO_2$

a) What is the useful product in this reaction? ....

b) Calculate the atom economy.

.... $atom\ economy = \dfrac{total\ M_r\ of\ useful\ products}{total\ M_r\ of\ reactants} \times 100$

....

c) What percentage of the starting materials are wasted?

....

Q2 It is important in industry to find the **best atom economy**.

a) Explain why. ....

....

....

b) What types of reaction have the highest atom economies? Give an example.

....

Q3 **Titanium** can be reduced from titanium chloride ($TiCl_4$) using magnesium or sodium.

a) Work out the atom economy for the reaction:

   i) with magnesium: $TiCl_4 + 2Mg \rightarrow Ti + 2MgCl_2$ ....

   ....

   ii) with sodium: $TiCl_4 + 4Na \rightarrow Ti + 4NaCl$ ....

   ....

b) Which one has the better atom economy? ....

Q4 **Chromium** can be extracted from its oxide (Cr_2O_3) using **aluminium**.
The products of the reaction are **aluminium oxide** and **chromium**.

Calculate the atom economy of this reaction.

....

....

Percentage Yield

Q1 James wanted to produce **silver chloride** (AgCl). He added a carefully measured mass of silver nitrate to an excess of dilute hydrochloric acid.

a) Write down the formula for calculating the **percentage yield** of a reaction?

....

b) James calculated that he should get 2.7 g of silver chloride, but he only got 1.2 g. What was the **percentage yield**?

....

Q2 Aaliya and Natasha mixed together barium chloride ($BaCl_2$) and sodium sulphate (Na_2SO_4) in a beaker. An **insoluble** substance formed. They **filtered** the solution to obtain the solid substance, and then transferred the solid to a clean piece of **filter paper** and left it to dry.

a) Aaliya calculated that they should produce a yield of **15 g** of barium sulphate. However, after completing the experiment they found they had only obtained **6 g**.

Calculate the **percentage yield** for this reaction.

....

b) Suggest two reasons why their actual yield was lower than their predicted yield.

1. ....

....

2. ....

....

Q3 The reaction between magnesium and oxygen produces a white powder, **magnesium oxide**. Four samples of magnesium, each weighing 2 g, were burned and the oxide produced was weighed. The **expected** yield was **3.33 g**.

Sample	Mass of oxide (g)
A	3.00
B	3.18
C	3.05
D	3.15

a) What is the percentage yield for each sample?

....

....

....

b) Which of the following are likely reasons why the yield was not 100%? Circle their letters.

A The reaction was too fast   **B** Too much magnesium was burned

C The magnesium was not pure   **D** Some of the oxide was lost before it was weighed

Percentage Yield

Q4 The reaction used to make **ammonia** by the **Haber process** is represented by the equation:

$$N_2 + 3H_2 \rightleftharpoons 2NH_3$$

a) What does the $\rightleftharpoons$ symbol mean? ....

b) Why will this reaction never give a 100% yield?

....

....

c) To get the best yield a low temperature is needed.
Suggest why a very low temperature is **not** used in industry.

....

Q5 Complete the table of results showing the **percentage yields** from different experiments.

You can use the space below for working out.

Yield	Expected yield	Percentage yield
3.4 g	4.0 g	**a)**
6.4 g	7.2 g	**b)**
3.6 g	**c)**	80%
d)	6.5 g	90%

Q6 Limestone is mainly **calcium carbonate**. If calcium carbonate is heated it leaves solid **calcium oxide**. When **100 tonnes** of limestone were heated, **42 tonnes** of calcium oxide were produced.

a) Write the equation for this reaction. ....

b) What was the expected yield?

Use a periodic table to help you with this question.

....

....

c) Using your answer from part b), calculate the percentage yield.

....

d) Why are you unlikely ever to get a 100% yield from this process?

....

....

C2 Topic 5 — Synthesis

C2 Topic 6 — In Your Element

Atoms

Q1   **Complete** the following sentences.

a)   Neutral atoms have a charge of ....

b)   A charged atom is called an ....

c)   A neutral atom has the same number of .... and ....

d)   If an electron is added to a neutral atom, the atom becomes .... charged.

Q2   **Complete** this table.

Particle	Mass	Charge
Proton	1	
	1	0
Electron		

Q3   **What is it?**

Choose from: **nucleus   proton   electron   neutron**

a)   It's in the centre of the atom and contains protons and neutrons. ....

b)   It moves around the nucleus in a shell.   ....

c)   It's the lightest.   ....

d)   It's relatively heavy and has no charge.   ....

Q4   Elements have a **mass number** and an **atomic number**.

a)   What does the **mass number** of an element tell you?

....

b)   What does the **atomic number** of an element tell you?

....

c)   Fill in this table, using a periodic table to help you.

Element	Symbol	Mass Number	Number of Protons	Number of Electrons	Number of Neutrons
Nitrogen	N		7		7
		32			16
Potassium				19	
	Cu		29		

Isotopes and Relative Atomic Mass

Q1   Choose the correct words to complete this paragraph.

| electrons | element | isotopes | protons | compound | neutrons |

.... are different atomic forms of the same .... which have

the same number of .... but different numbers of ....

Q2   Which of the following atoms are **isotopes** of each other? Explain how you know.

W $^{12}_{6}C$ **X** $^{40}_{18}Ar$ **Y** $^{14}_{6}C$ **Z** $^{40}_{20}Ca$

.... and .... because ....

Q3   **Carbon-14** is an unstable isotope of carbon.

a)   How many of the following particles does one atom of carbon-14 contain?

i) neutrons ....   **ii)** protons ....   **iii)** electrons ....

b)   Carbon-12 is the more common isotope of carbon.
Would you expect it to have different chemical properties from carbon-14? Explain your answer.

....

Q4   Draw lines to join the beginning of each sentence to its correct ending.

Relative atomic mass is

Relative abundance means

the proportion of one isotope in an element

the average mass of all atoms of that element

Q5   **Chlorine** has two main **isotopes**, ^{35}Cl and ^{37}Cl. Their relative abundances are shown in the table.

relative mass of isotope	relative abundance
35	3
37	1

Use this information to calculate the relative atomic mass of chlorine.

....

....

The Periodic Table

Q1 Choose from the elements given below to answer the following questions.

iodine   nickel   silicon   sodium   radon   krypton   calcium

a) Which two are in the same group? .... and ....

b) Name an alkali metal. ....

c) Name a noble gas. ....

d) Name an element with seven electrons in its outer shell. ....

e) Name a non-metal which is not in group 0. ....

Q2 **True** or **false?**

		True	False
a)	Elements in the same group have the same number of electrons in their outer shells.	☐	☐
b)	The periodic table shows the elements in order of ascending atomic mass.	☐	☐
c)	Each column in the periodic table contains elements with similar properties.	☐	☐
d)	The periodic table is made up of all the known compounds.	☐	☐
e)	There are more than 1000 known elements.	☐	☐

Q3 Some elements undergo **similar reactions** to each other.

a) Tick the pairs of elements that would undergo similar reactions.

A potassium and rubidium ☐   **C** calcium and oxygen ☐

B helium and fluorine ☐   **D** calcium and magnesium ☐

Stop copying...

b) Explain why elements in the **same group** undergo similar reactions.

....

....

Q4 Complete this table.

	Alternative Name for Group	Number of Electrons in Outer Shell
Group I	Alkali metals	
Group VII		7
Group 0		*

* excluding helium

Electron Shells

Q1 a) Tick the boxes to show whether each statement is **true** or **false**.

True False

  i) Electrons orbit the nucleus in energy levels called shells. ☐ ☐

  ii) The highest energy levels are always filled first. ☐ ☐

  iii) The lowest energy levels are closest to the nucleus. ☐ ☐

  iv) Atoms are most stable when they have partially filled shells. ☐ ☐

  v) A maximum of eight electrons can occupy the first shell. ☐ ☐

b) Write out corrected versions of the **false** statements.

....

....

....

Q2 Identify **two** things that are wrong with this diagram.

1. ....

2. ....

Q3 Write out the **electronic configurations** of the following elements.

a) Beryllium .... **d)** Calcium ....

b) Oxygen .... **e)** Aluminium ....

c) Silicon .... **f)** Argon ....

Q4 Are the following groups of elements **reactive** or **unreactive**? Explain why in each case.

a) Noble gases ....

....

b) Alkali metals ....

....

Q5 Describe the link between an element's position in the periodic table and the number of electrons it has in its outer shell.

....

....

Electron Shells

Q6   **Chlorine** has an atomic number of 17.

a)   What is its electron configuration?   ....

b)   Draw the electrons on the shells in the diagram.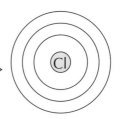

c)   Why does chlorine react readily?

....

Q7   Draw the **full electronic arrangements** for these elements. (The first three have been done for you.)

Hydrogen   Helium   Lithium

                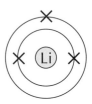

a) Carbon   **b)** Nitrogen   **c)** Fluorine

d) Sodium   **e)** Magnesium   **f)** Phosphorus

   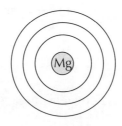   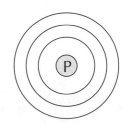

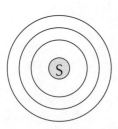   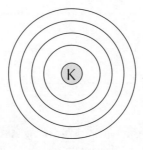   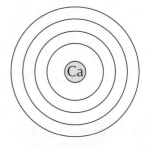

g) Sulphur   **h)** Potassium   **i)** Calcium

Top Tips: Once you've learnt the '**electron shell rules**' these are pretty easy — the first shell can only take **two** electrons, and the second and third shells a maximum of **eight** each. Don't forget it.

Ionic Bonding

Q1   **True** or **false**?   True   False

   a)   In ionic bonding, ions lose or gain electrons to give atoms.   ☐   ☐

   b)   Ions with opposite charges attract each other.   ☐   ☐

   c)   Elements that lose electrons form positive ions.   ☐   ☐

   d)   Elements that gain electrons form cations.   ☐   ☐

   e)   Atoms form ions so that they can have full outer shells.   ☐   ☐

Q2   Use the **diagram** to answer the following questions.

   a)   Which group of the periodic table does sodium belong to?   ....

   b)   How many electrons does chlorine need to gain in order to have a full outer shell?   ....

   c)   What is the charge on a sodium ion?   ....

   d)   What is the chemical formula of sodium chloride?   ....

Q3   Here are some **elements** and the **ions** they form:

Make sure the charges on the ions balance.

   beryllium, Be^{2+} potassium, K^+ iodine, I^- sulphur, S^{2-}

   Write down the formulae of four compounds which can be made using just these elements.

   1. ....

   2. ....

   3. ....

   4. ....

Ionic Bonding

Q4   Elements react in order to get a **full outer shell** of electrons.

a)   How many electrons does magnesium need to **lose** to get a full outer shell? ....

b)   How many electrons does oxygen need to **gain** to get a full outer shell?   ....

c)   Draw a 'dot and cross' diagram in the space provided to show what happens to the outer shells of electrons when magnesium and oxygen react.

The diagrams in question 2 are 'dot and cross' diagrams.

d)   What is the chemical formula of magnesium oxide? ....

Q5   Atoms can **gain** or **lose** electrons to get a full outer shell.

a)   How many electrons do the following elements need to **lose** in order to get a **full outer shell**?

   i) Lithium   ....   **ii)** Calcium   ....   **iii)** Potassium ....

b)   How many electrons do the following elements need to **gain** in order to get a **full outer shell**?

   i) Oxygen   ....   **ii)** Chlorine   ....   **iii)** Fluorine   ....

Q6   **Aluminium** is in **Group 3** of the periodic table.
Complete the following sentences by choosing the correct word from each pair.

a)   An atom of aluminium has **three** / **five** electrons in its outer shell.

b)   It will form an ion by **gaining** / **losing** these electrons.

c)   The charge on an aluminium ion will be **3+** / **3−**.

d)   The formula of the compound it makes with chloride ions (Cl^-) will be: **$AlCl_3$** / **Al_3Cl**.

e)   The formula of the compound it makes with oxide ions (O^{2-}) will be **Al_2O_3** / **Al_3O_2**.

Ionic Compounds

Q1 Use a 'dot and cross' diagram to show how **sodium** and **oxygen** react to give **sodium oxide**.

Q2 Explain how sodium and chlorine atoms react to form the ionic compound **sodium chloride**.

....

....

Q3 Use 'dot and cross' diagrams to explain why **potassium chloride** has the formula **KCl** but **magnesium chloride** has the formula **MgCl$_2$**.

Ionic Compounds

Q4 **Sodium chloride** (table salt) is a hard, crystalline substance.

a) What name is given to the arrangement of the atoms in a crystal of sodium chloride?

....

b) Why can't sodium chloride conduct electricity when it is solid?

....

c) Circle the correct words to explain why sodium chloride has a high melting point.

> Sodium chloride has very **strong** / **weak** chemical bonds between the
> **negative** / **positive** sodium ions and the **negative** / **positive** chlorine ions.
> This means that it needs a **small** / **large** amount of energy to break the bonds.

Q5 Mike carries out an experiment to find out if **potassium chloride** conducts electricity.
He tests the compound when it's solid, when it's dissolved in water and when it's molten.

a) Complete the following table of results.

	Conducts electricity?
When solid	
When dissolved in water	
When molten	

b) Explain your answers to part a).

....

....

....

Q6 The melting point of **calcium chloride** is **772 °C** and that of **carbon chloride** is **−23 °C**.

a) Which one is an ionic compound? Explain your choice.

....

b) Which one will conduct electricity when melted? Why does it conduct?

....

Reactivity Trends

Q1 Complete the paragraph below using words from the list.

outer electrons group same positively negatively inner shielded increases decreases

Atoms in the same .... of the periodic table have the .... number of .... in their outer shells. As you go down a group the distance between the .... electrons and the .... charged nucleus .... The outer electrons are said to be .... by the .... shells.

Q2 Draw lines to match up the three parts of each of the sentences below.

Alkali metals   do not form ions   because they have 7 electrons in their outer shells

Halogens   lose electrons   because they have full outer shells

Noble gases   gain electrons   because they have 1 electron in their outer shells

Q3 Diagrams 1, 2 and 3 show the outer electrons of three atoms from the **same group**.

a) Which group are the atoms from? ....

b) What do all of the above atoms need to do to form ions?

....

c) **i)** Which atom from this group would you expect to form an ion most easily? ....

ii) Why does it form ions more easily than the others? ....

....

Q4 Atoms of **lithium**, **sodium** and **potassium** have **3, 11** and **19 electrons** respectively.

a) Draw the electronic structure of each of these atoms in the space below.

b) State which of the three will be the most reactive and explain why.

....

....

Metals

Q1 The table shows the **properties** of some **elements**.

Element	Melting pt. (°C)	Boiling pt. (°C)	Electrical conductivity	Hardness
1	1903	2642	Good	Hard
2	114	444	None	Soft
3	1539	2887	Good	Hard
4	63	766	Good	Soft
5	3300	4827	Poor	Soft

Which of the elements 1 to 5 do you think are metals? ....

Q2 This table shows some of the **properties** of four different **metals**.

Metal	Heat conduction	Cost	Resistance to corrosion	Strength
1	average	high	excellent	good
2	average	medium	good	excellent
3	excellent	low	good	good
4	low	high	average	poor

Some metal is heavy.

Use the information in the table to choose which metal would be **best** for making:

a) Saucepan bases ....

b) Car bodies ....

c) A statue for a town centre ....

Think about how long a statue would have to last for.

Q3 All metals have a similar **structure**. This explains why many of them have similar **properties**.

a) Draw a labelled diagram of a typical metal structure, showing the electrons.

b) What is unusual about the electrons in a metal?

....

Metals

Q4   24-carat gold is **pure** gold. 9-carat gold contains **9 parts** gold to 15 parts other metal.
9-carat gold is **harder** and **cheaper** than 24-carat gold.

a)   What percentage of 9-carat gold is actually gold?

....

b)   Why is 9-carat gold harder than pure gold? ....

....

....

Q5   **Alloys** are very useful materials.

*Tonight Matthew,
I'm going to be...
steel.*

a)   Write a definition of the term **alloy**.

....

....

b)   Complete the following sentences about alloys using the metals below.

iron   copper   silver   tin   titanium

i)   Bronze is an alloy that contains copper and ....

ii) Cupronickel, which is used in 'silver' coins, contains nickel and ....

iii) Steel is an alloy made from carbon and ....

c)   Give an example of how alloying a metal can change its properties.

....

....

Q6   **Gold** can be hammered into a sheet (called gold leaf) that's so **thin** you can see through it.
Complete the following sentences by circling the correct word in each pair.

a)   Gold leaf can be made because gold is very **malleable** / **tactile**.

b)   Thin sheets of glass have to be made by pouring molten glass because glass is **malleable** / **brittle**.

c)   Metals are malleable because the layers of **molecules** / **atoms** can slide over each other.

Top Tips: There are just two things that are really important here — the structure and
properties of metals. Make sure you know how the structure of a metal is related to its properties,
and also about how you can mix a metal with other things to change its properties. Easy peasy.

Electrolysis and the Half-Equations

Q1   Draw lines to join these words with their correct meanings.

Electrolysis

Electrolyte

Anode

Cathode

Cation

Anion

The positive electrode.

The breakdown of a substance using electricity.

Positive ion that is attracted to the cathode.

Negative ion that is attracted to the anode.

The negative electrode.

The liquid that is used in electrolysis.

Q2   Are these statements about the extraction of **aluminium** true or false?

		True	False
a)	Substances can only be electrolysed if molten or in solution.	☐	☐
b)	In the extraction of aluminium the electrolyte is molten aluminium metal.	☐	☐
c)	Aluminium is extracted from its ore, bauxite.	☐	☐
d)	Oxygen gas is given off during the extraction of aluminium by electrolysis.	☐	☐
e)	Aluminium is collected at the anode.	☐	☐

Q3   From the substances listed in the box below, write down those that:

copper,   copper sulphate crystals,   dilute sulphuric acid,   seawater,   alcohol,   table salt

a)   can never be electrolysed ....

b)   can be electrolysed as they are ....

c)   can only be electrolysed when melted or dissolved in water

....

Q4   Complete this table to show the results of the **electrolysis** of some **molten substances**.

Salt	Anode product	Cathode product
Sodium chloride		
Calcium iodide		
Silver bromide		

Electrolysis and the Half-Equations

Q5 The diagram below shows the electrolysis of **molten aluminium oxide**.

molten aluminium oxide

Write the labels that should go at points A–G:

A ....

B ....

C ....

D ....

E ....

F ....

G ....

Q6 **Lead bromide** is an ionic substance. It doesn't easily dissolve in water.

a) How could lead bromide be made into a liquid for electrolysis?

....

b) Write **balanced** half-equations for the processes that occur at the cathode and anode during the electrolysis of lead bromide.

Cathode: ....

Anode: ....

Lead ions have a 2+ charge. And remember, bromide ions pair up to become bromine molecules (Br$_2$).

Q7 Write **half-equations** to show what happens at each electrode when these salts are electrolysed.

a) Potassium chloride, KCl

Cathode: .... Anode: ....

b) Calcium bromide, CaBr$_2$

Cathode: .... Anode: ....

c) Sodium fluoride, NaF

Cathode: .... Anode: ....

Top Tips: All I can say is, don't get the **cathode** and the **anode** mixed up. The cathode is the **negative** electrode and it attracts the **cations**, which are the positive ions. The anode is **positive** and so attracts **anions**, which are negative. It's easy to get confused, so make sure you know it properly now.

Mixed Questions — C2 Topics 5 & 6

Q1   Carbon contains the isotopes **carbon-12** and **carbon-14**.

a)   Write down the number of **protons**, **electrons** and **neutrons** in carbon-12.

.... protons   .... neutrons   .... electrons

b)   Most cars burn fuels containing carbon. The exhaust gases from the engine contain small amounts of carbon monoxide, CO.

i)   Calculate the relative formula mass of carbon monoxide.

....

ii)   Carbon monoxide reacts slowly with oxygen, O_2, to form carbon dioxide, CO_2.

$$2CO \text{ (g)} \ + \ O_2 \text{ (g)} \ \rightarrow \ 2CO_2 \text{ (g)}$$

If 280 g of CO reacts with excess oxygen, what mass of **carbon dioxide** will be produced?

....

....

Q2   **Ethene** (C_2H_4) is an **unsaturated** molecule.

a)   i)   Draw the structure of a molecule of ethene, showing all the bonds.

ii)   Describe a test that would distinguish between ethane and ethene.
Give the result of the test for each substance.

....

....

b)   **Hydrogenated vegetable oils** are used in many foods. Explain what 'hydrogenation' means.

....

c)   Which of the following best explains why vegetable oils are hydrogenated? Circle one letter.

A It makes the oils better for your health.   B It gives the oils a firmer consistency.

C It gives the oils a more appealing taste.   D It makes the oils look more appetising.

Q3   Drug companies use **staged synthesis** to make a 'family' of very similar compounds.
These can then all be tested at once to see if any of them will make an **effective drug**.
Explain the advantage of doing this.

....

....

Mixed Questions — C2 Topics 5 & 6

Q4   The table shows the **uses** of some different **plastics** and the **monomers** used to make them.

monomer		polymer	use for polymer
ethene	$\underset{H}{\overset{H}{>}}C=C\underset{H}{\overset{H}{<}}$	poly(ethene) $\left(\begin{matrix}H & H \\ C-C \\ H & H\end{matrix}\right)_n$	
propene	$\underset{H}{\overset{H}{>}}C=C\underset{CH_3}{\overset{H}{<}}$		rope
styrene	$\underset{H}{\overset{H}{>}}C=C\underset{O}{\overset{H}{<}}$		

a)   Complete the table.

b)   Polythene is a flexible plastic. Explain what this tells you about the forces between its molecules.

....

c)   Would you expect polythene to have a low or a high melting point? Explain your answer.

....

Q5   8.1 g of a compound contains 4.9 g magnesium and 3.2 g oxygen. What is its **empirical formula**?

....

....

Q6   The first three elements in **Group I** of the **periodic table** are lithium, sodium and potassium.

a)   Write down the electron configurations for these three elements. (Use the periodic table to help you.)

....

b)   Describe and explain how the reactivity of these elements changes as you move down the group.

....

....

Q7   **Fermentation** is used to produce alcohol from sugars: $C_6H_{12}O_6 \rightarrow 2C_2H_5OH + 2CO_2$.
Calculate the **atom economy** of this reaction.

....

....

Mixed Questions — C2 Topics 5 & 6

Q8 Crude oil is a mixture of **saturated** and **unsaturated hydrocarbons**.

a) Ethane (C_2H_6) is a saturated hydrocarbon.

   i) Draw the structure of a molecule of ethane, showing all the bonds.

   ii) What are saturated hydrocarbons known as? ....

b) Short-chain hydrocarbons like ethane and ethene can be made from less useful long-chain hydrocarbons. Explain how this is done in industry (including the reaction conditions).

   ....

   ....

Q9 **Properties** of materials are related to the type of **bonding** in the molecules.

a) Explain why **iron** is strong and conducts electricity.

   ....

   ....

b) Explain how the properties of **sodium chloride** are related to the bonding within it.

   ....

   ....

Q10 An **electric current** is passed through **liquid lead bromide**, as shown in the diagram.

a) What is this process called?

   ....

b) Why does the lead bromide have to be liquid?

   ....

   ....

c) Lead bromide, $PbBr_2$, is composed of Pb^{2+} and Br^- ions.

   i) State which ion moves toward each electrode during this process.

   Electrode A ....   Electrode B ....

   ii) Balance the following half equations for the reactions.

   $$Pb^{2+} + \quad e^- \rightarrow \quad Pb \qquad\qquad Br^- \rightarrow \quad Br_2 + \quad e^-$$

Covalent Bonding

Q1 Indicate whether each statement below is **true** or **false**.

		True	False
a)	Covalent bonding involves sharing electrons.	☐	☐
b)	Atoms with a full outer shell are more stable.	☐	☐
c)	Some atoms can make both ionic and covalent bonds.	☐	☐
d)	A hydrogen atom can form two covalent bonds.	☐	☐
e)	A carbon atom can form four covalent bonds.	☐	☐

Q2 **Complete** the following table to show how many extra electrons are needed to **fill up** the **outer shells** of these atoms.

Atom	Carbon	Chlorine	Hydrogen	Nitrogen
Number of electrons needed to fill outer shell				

Q3 Complete the following diagrams by adding **electrons** to the outer shells.

a) Hydrogen chloride (HCl)

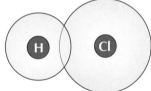

b) Hydrogen (H$_2$)

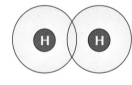

c) Carbon dioxide (CO$_2$)

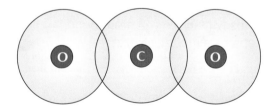

d) Water (H$_2$O)

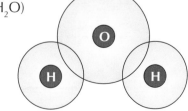

Covalent Bonding

Q4   The **structural formula** of methane is shown in the diagram.

a)   What **can't** the structural formula tell you about the structure of a molecule?

....

....

b)   What type of diagram of a methane molecule would give you extra information?

....

c)   Why might it be important to have this extra information?

....

Q5   **Oxygen** atoms make **covalent bonds** with atoms of various elements.

a)   How many extra electrons does an atom gain by making a single covalent bond?   ....

b)   How many electrons are there in the outer shell of an oxygen atom?   ....

c)   How many more electrons does an oxygen atom need to gain in order to fill its outer shell?

....

d)   How many covalent bonds must an oxygen atom make to have a full outer shell of electrons?

....

Q6   Atoms form bonds to gain a **full outer shell** of electrons.

a)   Hydrogen atoms can only make one covalent bond.

How many hydrogen atoms will an oxygen atom bond
with before it has a full outer shell of electrons?

....

b)   A molecule of carbon dioxide contains just one carbon atom and two oxygen atoms,
yet carbon atoms need to gain a total of four electrons to fill their outer shells.

Explain how these atoms bond together so that they all have full outer shells of electrons.

....

....

> **_Top Tips:_**   You need to know why some elements bond covalently and what **properties**
> molecules have when they've bonded this way. Those dot and cross diagrams are pretty important too.

Molecular Substances: the Halogens

Q1 Fill in the blanks in the following paragraph by choosing words from the list.

weak   hard   small   easy   large   strong

Simple molecular substances are made from .... molecules. The covalent bonds

that hold the atoms together are .... but the forces between the molecules are quite

.... Because of this it is fairly .... to separate the molecules.

Q2 Hydrogen and chlorine share electrons to form a molecule called **hydrogen chloride**.

Predict two properties that hydrogen chloride will have.

1. ....

2. ....

Q3 Complete the following sentences by circling the correct option, and explain your answers.

a) The melting and boiling points of simple molecular substances are **low / high**.

....

b) Simple molecular substances **conduct / don't conduct** electricity.

....

Q4 The table below shows the **atomic numbers** and **melting points** for three **halogens**.

Halogen	Atomic no.	Melting pt.
Fluorine	9	$-220\,°C$
Bromine	35	$-7\,°C$
Iodine	53	$114\,°C$

a) Plot the data on the axes given.

b) Describe the relationship between atomic number and melting point for the halogens.

....

....

c) Explain fully why this relationship exists.

....

....

Giant Covalent Structures: Carbon

Q1 Circle the correct words to complete the following paragraph.

Giant covalent structures contain **charged ions** / **uncharged atoms**. The covalent bonds between the atoms are **strong** / **weak**. Giant covalent structures have **high** / **low** melting points and they are usually **soluble** / **insoluble** in water.

Q2 **Graphite** and **diamond** are both made entirely from **carbon**, but have different properties.

a) Explain why graphite is a good conductor of electricity.

....

....

b) Explain how diamond's structure makes it hard.

....

....

Q3 A molecule of **buckminsterfullerene** is made up of 60 carbon atoms.

a) What is the **molecular formula** of buckminsterfullerene? ....

b) How many covalent bonds does each carbon atom form? ....

c) Can buckminsterfullerene conduct electricity? Explain your answer.

....

....

Q4 The different **forms** of carbon have different **properties** and **uses**. From the list, select a suitable use for the following forms of carbon. State the property that justifies your choice.

glass-cutting tool   computer chips   pencils

a) **Fullerene nanotube** Use: ....

Property: ....

b) **Graphite** Use: ....

Property: ....

c) **Diamond** Use: ....

Property: ....

Treatment and Homeopathy

Q1 If you were conducting a **trial** of a new drug to test its effectiveness and safety, which of the following questions would you set out to answer? Tick one or more boxes.

A ☐ Do people like the taste of the drug?

B ☐ Do people get better after taking the drug?

C ☐ How much does the drug cost?

D ☐ Does the drug cause any serious side effects?

Taster, madam?

Q2 Draw lines to match the following terms to the sentence that best describes them.

Placebo

Homeopathic remedy

Control group

A highly diluted natural substance

A set of patients taking a placebo

A control 'medicine' which does not actually contain any drug

Q3 In order to test the **effectiveness** of a drug, a researcher gives the drug to a group of patients over a period of time and then carries out interviews to see if their condition has improved.

a) Why is this not a fair test of the drug?

....

b) Explain fully how you would improve the trial to make it a fair test.

....

....

....

c) What is meant by the 'placebo effect'?

....

....

Top Tips: Make sure you know all about placebos and drug testing — it's a vital part of making drugs (and answering exam questions). Homeopathic remedies are just as important here, too.

Treatment and Homeopathy

Q4   Homeopathic remedies are one type of alternative to conventional medicine.

a)   Put the following stages in the preparation of a homeopathic remedy into the correct order.

    A The solution is diluted with water.   **B** The last two steps are repeated many times.

    C The solution is shaken.   **D** A chemical is extracted from a plant, animal or mineral.

    E The active ingredient is dissolved in alcohol.   **Order:** ....

b)   What do homeopaths believe happens when the mixture is shaken?

....

c)   Why don't homeopathic remedies have to go through the same testing process as other medicines?

....

d)   Why do many scientists find it difficult to believe that homeopathic remedies really work?

....

....

Q5   In a **trial** designed to test the effectiveness of a **homeopathic cold remedy**, 100 people with a cold are given a drink. Fifty of the drinks contain the homeopathic remedy and fifty are **placebos**.

None of the volunteers know which they've been given. **Two days** later everyone is asked if they are feeling better. The results of the trial are summarised in the table.

Control group		Group taking remedy	
No. feeling better	No. not feeling better	No. feeling better	No. not feeling better
31	19	32	18

a)   What percentage of the control group felt better after one week?

....

b)   What percentage of the group taking the real remedy felt better after one week?

....

c)   Suggest why some people in the control group (who took no remedy) felt better after one week.

....

d)   Does the trial show that this remedy is effective? Explain your answer.

....

....

e)   How could this trial be improved to give more reliable results?

....

Rates of Reaction

Q1 Circle the correct words to complete the statements below about **rates of reaction**.

a) The **higher** / **lower** the temperature, the faster the rate of a reaction.

b) A **higher** / **lower** concentration will reduce the rate of a reaction.

c) If the reactants are **gases** / **liquids**, a higher pressure will give a **faster** / **slower** reaction.

d) A smaller particle size **increases** / **decreases** the rate of reaction.

e) A catalyst changes the rate of reaction but **is** / **isn't** used up.

Q2 In an experiment, **different sizes** of marble chips were reacted with excess hydrochloric acid. The **same mass** of marble was used each time. The graph below shows how much **gas** was produced when using large marble chips (X), medium marble chips (Y) and small marble chips (Z).

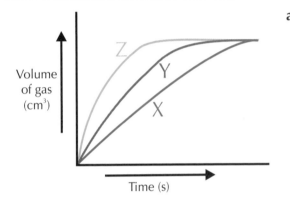

a) i) Which curve (X, Y or Z) shows the **fastest** reaction? Circle the correct answer.

 X Y Z

ii) How can you tell this by looking at the graph?

....

....

....

b) Why was an **excess** of acid used? ....

c) Why do all the reactions produce the **same** volume of gas?

....

d) On the graph, draw the curve you would expect to see if you used **more** of the small marble chips. Assume that all the other conditions are the same as before.

Q3 Another experiment investigated the **change in mass** of the reactants during a reaction in which a **gas** was given off. The graph below shows the results for three experiments carried out under different conditions.

a) Suggest **why** reaction R involved a greater change in mass than reactions P and Q.

....

....

b) What might have caused the difference between reaction P and reaction Q?

....

....

Measuring Rates of Reaction

Q1   Use the words provided to complete the sentences below about **measuring rates of reaction**.

    faster   speed   volume   reactants   gas   mass   formed   precipitation

a)   The .... of a reaction can be measured by observing either how quickly

the .... are used up or how quickly the products are ....

b)   In a .... reaction you usually measure how quickly the product is formed.

The product turns the solution cloudy. The .... it turns cloudy the faster

the reaction.

c)   In a reaction that produces a .... you can measure how quickly the

.... of the reactants changes or measure the .... of gas

given off in a certain time interval.

Q2   Sam conducted two experiments with equal masses of marble chips and equal
volumes of hydrochloric acid (HCl). He used two **different concentrations** of acid
and measured the **change in mass** of the reactants. Below is a graph of the results.

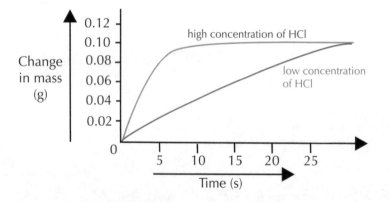

acid concentration

Circle the letter(s) to show the valid conclusion(s) you might draw **from this graph**.

A   Rate of reaction depends on the temperature of the reactants.

B   Increasing the concentration of the acid has no effect on the rate of reaction.

C   Rate of reaction depends on the acid concentration.

D   Rate of reaction depends on the mass of the marble chips.

Top Tips: It's a pretty good idea to learn the four things that reaction rate depends on, and it's
not a bad idea to know the formula for calculating rate of reaction. Remember, graphs can be used to
show reaction speeds, and there's also three methods of measuring reactions that you should know.

Measuring Rates of Reaction

Q3 Charlie was comparing the rate of reaction of 5 g of magnesium ribbon with 20 ml of **five different concentrations** of hydrochloric acid. Each time he measured how much **gas** was produced during the **first minute** of the reaction. He did the experiment **twice** for each concentration of acid and obtained these results:

Concentration of HCl (mol/dm³)	Experiment 1 — volume of gas produced (cm³)	Experiment 2 — volume of gas produced (cm³)	Average volume of gas produced (cm³)
2	92	96	
1.5	63	65	
1	44	47	
0.5	20	50	
0.25	9	9	

a) Fill in the last column of the table.

b) Circle the **anomalous** result in the table.

c) Which concentration of hydrochloric acid produced the fastest rate of reaction? ....

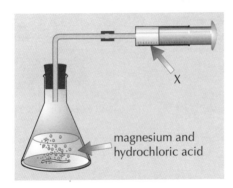

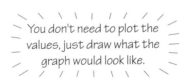
magnesium and hydrochloric acid

d) A diagram of the **apparatus** used in the experiment is shown on the left.

  i) What is the object marked **X** called?

  ....

  ii) Name one other key piece of apparatus needed for this experiment (not shown in the diagram).

  ....

e) **Sketch** a graph of the average volume of gas produced against concentration of HCl and **label** the axes. Do not include the anomalous result.

You don't need to plot the values, just draw what the graph would look like.

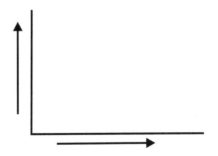

f) Why did Charlie do the experiment twice and calculate the average volume?

....

g) How might the anomalous result have come about?

....

h) Suggest two changes Charlie could make to improve his results if he repeated his investigation.

1. ....

2. ....

Collision Theory

Q1   Circle the correct words to complete the sentences.

a)   In order for a reaction to occur, the particles must **remain still** / **collide**.

b)   If you heat up a reaction mixture, you give the particles more **energy** / **surface area**.

c)   This makes them move **faster** / **more slowly** and so there is **more** / **less** chance of successful collisions.

d)   So, increasing the temperature increases the **concentration** / **rate** of reaction.

Q2   Draw lines to match up the **changes** with their **effects**.

| increasing the temperature | | provides a surface for particles to stick to and lowers activation energy |

| decreasing the concentration | | makes the particles move faster, so they collide more often |

| adding a catalyst | | gives particles a bigger area of solid reactant to react with |

| increasing the surface area | | means fewer particles of reactant are present, so fewer collisions occur |

Q3   Gases are always under **pressure**.

a)   **i)**   If you increase the pressure on a gas reaction, does the rate of reaction **increase** or **decrease**?

....

ii)   Explain your answer. ....

....

....

b)   In the boxes on the right draw two diagrams — one showing particles of two different gases at low pressure, the other showing the same two gases at high pressure.

low pressure   high pressure

Q4   Here are four statements about **surface area** and **rates of reaction**. Tick the appropriate boxes to show whether they are true or false.

True   False

a)   Breaking a larger solid into smaller pieces decreases its surface area.   ☐ ☐

b)   A larger surface area means a faster rate of reaction.   ☐ ☐

c)   A larger surface area decreases the number of useful collisions.   ☐ ☐

d)   Powdered marble has a larger surface area than an equal mass of marble chips has.   ☐ ☐

Q5   Explain what a catalyst is and what it does.

....

....

Catalysts

Q1   To get a reaction to **start**, you have to give the particles some **energy**.

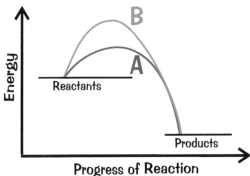

a)   What is this energy called? Underline the correct answer.

potential energy   activation energy   chemical energy

b)   The diagram opposite shows two reactions —
one with a catalyst and one without. Which
line shows the reaction **with** a catalyst? ....

c)   On this diagram, draw and label arrows to show the
activation energy for the reaction without a catalyst and
the activation energy for the reaction with a catalyst.

Q2   Solid catalysts come in **different forms**. Two examples are **pellets** and **fine gauze**.

Explain why solid catalysts are used in forms such as these.

....

....

Q3   Industrial catalysts are often **metals**.

You find them in the middle
of the periodic table.

a)   Which type of metal is commonly used? ....

b)   Give an example of a metal catalyst and say which industrial process it is used in.

....

Q4   This question is about **enzymes**.

a)   Underline **two** of the following descriptions that can be used to correctly describe an enzyme.

A A transition metal   **B** A biological catalyst   **C** A protein   **D** An element

b)   Reactions in living organisms are catalysed by enzymes. Give two advantages of this.

....

....

c)   Give the optimum temperature and pH for a **typical** human enzyme.

....

d)   Explain what would happen to this enzyme if the temperature rose too far above the optimum.

....

....

Energy Transfer in Reactions

Q1 Circle the correct words in this paragraph.

Exothermic / endothermic reactions take in energy, usually in the form of heat / sound.

This is often shown by a fall in temperature / mass.

Q2 Two examples of exothermic reactions are **burning fuels** and **neutralisation reactions**.

a) Write **B** for burning fuel or **N** for neutralisation reaction next to each of the following reactions.

☐ hydrochloric acid + sodium hydroxide → sodium chloride + water

☐ methanol + oxygen → carbon dioxide + water

☐ potassium hydroxide + sulphuric acid → potassium sulphate + water

☐ butane + oxygen → carbon dioxide + water

b) Give another word for 'burning'. ....

Q3 State whether bond **breaking** and bond **forming** are exothermic or endothermic reactions, and explain why in both cases.

Bond breaking ....

....

Bond forming ....

....

Q4 Limestone (**calcium carbonate**, $CaCO_3$) decomposes when heated to form quicklime (calcium oxide, CaO) and carbon dioxide.

a) Write a balanced symbol equation for this reaction.

....

b) The reaction requires a large amount of heat.

i) Is it **exothermic** or **endothermic**? ....

ii) Explain your answer. ....

c) Decomposing 1 tonne (1000 kg) of $CaCO_3$ requires about 1 800 000 kJ of heat energy.

i) How much heat energy would be needed to make **1 kg** of $CaCO_3$ decompose?

....

ii) How much $CaCO_3$ could be decomposed by **90 000 kJ** of heat energy?

....

Energy Transfer in Reactions

Q5   When **methane** burns in oxygen it forms carbon dioxide and water. The bonds in the methane and oxygen molecules **break** and new bonds are formed to make carbon dioxide and water molecules.

a)   Is energy taken in or given out when the bonds in the methane and oxygen molecules break?

....

b)   Is energy taken in or given out when the bonds in the carbon dioxide and water molecules form?

....

c)   Methane is a fuel commonly used in cooking and heating. Do you think that burning methane is an exothermic or an endothermic process? Explain your answer.

....

....

d)   Which of the following statements about burning methane is true? Circle one letter.

A **The energy involved in breaking bonds is greater than the energy involved in forming bonds.**

B **The energy involved in breaking bonds is less than the energy involved in forming bonds.**

C **The energy involved in breaking bonds is the same as the energy involved in forming bonds.**

Q6   Here are some practical uses of chemical reactions. Decide whether each reaction is **endothermic** or **exothermic**. In the box, put **N** for endothermic and **X** for exothermic.

a)   A camping stove burns methylated spirit to heat a pan of beans. ☐

b)   Special chemical cool packs are used by athletes to treat injuries. They are placed on the skin and draw heat away from the injury. ☐

c)   Self-heating cans of coffee contain chemicals in the base. When the chemicals are combined they produce heat which warms the can. ☐

d)   Baking powder is used to make cakes rise. When it's heated in the oven it thermally decomposes to produce a gas. ☐

Top Tips: Anything that takes heat in is **endothermic**. Endothermic reactions are not unusual in everyday life — think about what happens when you cook eggs and use baking powder.

Reversible Reactions

Q1   Use words from the list below to complete the following sentences about **reversible reactions**.

escape   reactants   catalysts   closed   products   react   balance

a)   In a reversible reaction, the .... of the reaction can themselves

.... to give the original ....

b)   At equilibrium, the amounts of reactants and products reach a ....

c)   To reach equilibrium the reaction must happen in a .... system,

where products and reactants can't ....

Q2   Look at this diagram of a **reversible reaction**.

a)   For the forward reaction:

i)   give the reactant(s)   ....

ii)   give the product(s)   ....

b)   Here are two labels:

> **X** product splits up
>
> **Y** reactants combine

The reaction going from left to right is called the forward reaction. The reaction going from right to left is called the backward reaction.

i)   Which of these labels goes in position 1 — X or Y?   ....

ii)   Which goes in position 2 — X or Y?   ....

c)   Write the equation for the reversible reaction. ....

d)   Complete the sentence by circling the correct phrase.

In a dynamic equilibrium, the forward and backward reactions are happening:

at different rates / at zero rate / at the same rate.

Q3   Which of these statements about reversible reactions are **true** and which are **false**?

		True	False
a)	The position of an equilibrium depends on the reaction conditions.	☐	☐
b)	Upon reaching a dynamic equilibrium, the reactions stop taking place.	☐	☐
c)	You can move the position of equilibrium to get more product.	☐	☐
d)	At equilibrium there will always be equal quantities of products and reactants.	☐	☐

C2 Topic 8 — How Fast? How Furious?

Reversible Reactions

Q4 Substances A and B react to produce substances C and D in a **reversible reaction**.

$$2A_{(g)} + B_{(g)} \rightleftharpoons 2C_{(g)} + D_{(g)}$$

a) Give two reaction conditions which often affect the **position of equilibrium**.

1. ....   2. ....

b) The forward reaction is **exothermic**. Does the backward reaction give out or take in heat?
Explain your answer.

....

....

c) If the temperature is raised, does the **forward** or **backward** reaction increase? ....

d) Explain why changing the temperature of a reversible reaction always affects the position
of the equilibrium.

....

e) What effect will changing the **pressure** have on the position
of equilibrium in this reaction? Explain your answer.

....

Q5 Look at the equation showing another **reversible reaction** below.

a) In this reaction:

$$2SO_{2(g)} + O_{2(g)} \rightleftharpoons 2SO_{3(g)}$$

i) Which reaction, forward or backward, is accompanied by a **decrease** in volume?
Explain your answer.

....

ii) How will increasing the pressure affect the position of equilibrium in this reaction?

....

b) What does adding a catalyst to a reversible reaction do?
Circle the letter next to the correct answer.

A   It moves the equilibrium position towards the products.

B   It makes the reaction reach equilibrium more quickly.

C   It moves the equilibrium position towards the reactants.

D   It causes a decrease in pressure.

c) What happens to the amount of product at equilibrium when you use a catalyst?

....

The Haber Process

Q1 The Haber process is used to make **ammonia**. The equation for the reaction is:

$$N_2(g) + 3H_2(g) \rightleftharpoons 2NH_3(g)$$

a) Name the reactants in the forward reaction. ....

b) Which side of the equation has more molecules? ....

c) How should the pressure be changed in order to produce more ammonia? Explain your answer.

....

Q2 The **industrial conditions** for the Haber process are carefully chosen.

a) What conditions are used? Tick one box.

| ☐ **1000 atmospheres, 450 °C** | ☐ **200 atmospheres, 1000 °C** | ☐ **450 atmospheres, 200 °C** | ☐ **200 atmospheres, 450 °C** |

b) Give two reasons why the pressure used is chosen.

1. ....

2. ....

Q3 In the Haber process reaction, the **forward** reaction is **exothermic**.

a) What effect will raising the temperature have on the **amount** of ammonia formed?

....

b) Explain why a high temperature is used industrially.

....

c) What happens to the leftover nitrogen and hydrogen? ....

Q4 **Ammonium nitrate** is used by farmers as a fertiliser.

a) Fill in the blanks to show the reactants used to produce ammonium nitrate.

.... + ... → **ammonium nitrate**

b) Explain why it makes a good fertiliser. ....

....

c) Give **one advantage** and **one disadvantage** of using artificial fertilisers like ammonium nitrate in farming, rather then using organic alternatives.

....

....

....

Mixed Questions — C2 Topics 7 & 8

Q1 The bonding and electron arrangement in a molecule of **silane, SiH₄**, is similar to that in **methane**.

a) What type of bonding is present in methane?

....

b) Draw a diagram to show the electron arrangement in **silane** in the box provided.

Q2 **Iodine** exists as simple **diatomic molecules**, I₂.

a) Explain why iodine has a low melting point. ....

....

b) Predict whether iodine is likely to be able to conduct electricity. Justify your prediction.

....

c) Why do the melting and boiling points of the halogens increase as you go down the group?

....

....

Q3 The following questions concern three forms of **carbon** — **diamond**, **graphite** and **buckminsterfullerene**. Diamond's melting point is 3550 °C and graphite's is 3652 °C.

a) Explain why graphite and diamond have very high melting points.

....

....

b) Explain why buckminsterfullerene and graphite conduct electricity, but diamond does not.

....

....

Q4 **Homeopathic remedies** contain diluted doses of natural substances that produce symptoms of illness. However, unlike conventional medicines, they do **not** have to be rigorously tested.

a) Explain why this is. ....

....

b) People who take homeopathic medicines often feel better, even though there is little scientific evidence that the medicine itself has any physical effect. Suggest a **scientific** explanation for this.

....

Mixed Questions — C2 Topics 7 & 8

Q5 The results of a reaction between **calcium carbonate** and **hydrochloric acid** are shown on the graph.

a) The products of this reaction are calcium chloride (which forms a colourless solution), water and carbon dioxide. Suggest how the rate of this reaction could be measured.

....

....

volume of gas / cm³ curve with points A, B, C rising to 35 °C plateau; axis time / s

b) Which part of the curve shows the fastest rate of reaction — A, B or C? ....

c) Explain what happens to the reaction at point C.

....

d) At 35 °C, the reaction followed the curve shown on the graph. Draw two other curves on the same diagram to show how the rate of reaction might change at 25 °C and 45 °C.

e) Give three factors other than temperature on which the rate of reaction depends.

....

Q6 **Ammonium nitrate** is an artificial fertiliser formed from a reaction between ammonia and nitric acid.

a) Outline the environmental and health problems that may be caused by widespread use of ammonium nitrate.

....

....

....

b) What can farmers do to help avoid these problems?

....

Q7 In many reactions, a **catalyst** can be used to increase the **reaction rate**.

a) Explain how a catalyst works.

....

....

b) Which form would be better as a catalyst, a stick or a powder? Explain your answer.

....

....

Mixed Questions — C2 Topics 7 & 8

Q8 **Iodine** vapour reacts with **hydrogen** to form hydrogen iodide.
The reaction is **endothermic** and the mixture turns from purple to colourless.

$$I — I \quad + \quad H — H \quad \longrightarrow \quad 2(H — I)$$

a) Which old bonds are broken? ....

b) Which new bonds are made? ....

c) Which of the processes is endothermic — breaking bonds or forming new ones?

....

d) Do you think that the temperature of the reaction vessel will rise or fall during this reaction? Explain your answer.

....

e) What effect does lowering the activation energy (by using a catalyst) have on a reaction?

....

Q9 The **thermal decomposition** of ammonium chloride is a **reversible reaction**.

$$NH_4Cl\,(s) \quad \underset{\text{exothermic}}{\overset{\text{endothermic}}{\rightleftharpoons}} \quad NH_3\,(g) \ + \ HCl\,(g)$$

a) In which direction will the equilibrium move if the temperature is increased?

....

b) In which direction will the equilibrium move if the pressure is increased?

....

Q10 The rate of a chemical reaction can be **increased** by using a **catalyst** or increasing the **temperature**.

a) What catalyst is used in the Haber process?

....

b) The Haber process takes place at a temperature of 450 °C. By considering the effect on the yield and the rate of reaction, explain why a catalyst is used rather than using a higher temperature.

....

....

....

P2 Topic 9 — As Fast As You Can

Speed and Velocity

Q1   A pulse of **laser light** takes **1.3 seconds** to travel from the Moon to the Earth. The **speed of light** is approximately 3×10^8 **m/s**.

You'll need to rearrange the speed formula.

How far away is the Moon from the Earth? Give your answer in km.

....

Q2   Tom starts his journey to school by **walking** to the bus stop — this takes **10 minutes** at a speed of **1 m/s**. Next, Tom catches the **bus** and travels for **20 minutes** at an average speed of **15 m/s**. Tom usually has to **run** the last bit of the journey, which takes **5 minutes** at an average speed of **3 m/s**.

a)   How many seconds does each part of Tom's journey take?

....

....

b)   How far does Tom travel in total?

....

....

c)   What is Tom's average speed for the whole journey? Assume there's no wait at the bus stop.

....

Q3   **Speed cameras** can be used to catch speeding motorists. The section of road in the diagram below has a **speed limit** of **50 miles per hour**.

a)   1 mile = 1609 metres. Show that 50 miles per hour is about the same speed as 22 m/s.

....

b)   The diagram below shows a car passing in front of a speed camera. The two pictures show the position of the car 0.5 s apart. The distance between each white line on the road is 5 metres.

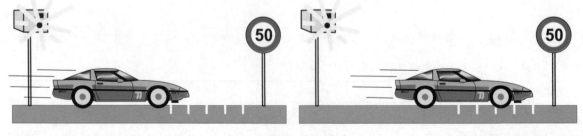

Was the car breaking the speed limit? Show your working.

....

Top Tips: Speed and velocity are both how fast you're going, and are calculated in the same way. The only difference between speed and velocity is that velocity has direction. Simple.

Speed and Velocity

Q4   Ealing is about **12 km** west of Marble Arch. It takes a
tube train **20 minutes** to get to Marble Arch from Ealing.

Only **one** of the following statements is true. Circle the appropriate letter.

    A   The average speed of the train is 60 m/s.

    B   The average velocity of the train is 10 m/s.

    C   The average velocity of the train is 60 m/s due east.

    D   The average speed of the train is 10 m/s.

    E   The average velocity of the train is 10 m/s due west.

Q5   A **hare** challenges a **tortoise** to a **race**. The hare is so confident he'll win that he
takes a nap on the way — he sleeps too long and the tortoise ends up winning.
Here are some facts and figures about the race:

The **tortoise** ran at a constant speed of **5 m/s** throughout the race — pretty impressive.

The **hare** ran at **10 m/s** for **300 s** before falling asleep. He slept for **600 s** and then carried on at
10 m/s towards the finish line.

The length of the **race track** was **5000 m**.

a)   How far did the hare travel before falling asleep?

....

b)   Add the information about the hare's run to the graph below.

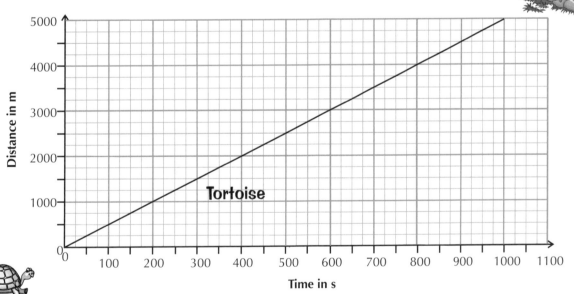

c)   When did the tortoise overtake the hare?

....

d)   How long did the tortoise have to wait at the finish line before the hare arrived?

....

Acceleration and Velocity-Time Graphs

Q1   An egg is dropped from the top of the Eiffel tower.
It hits the ground after **8 seconds**, at a speed of **80 m/s**.

    a)   Calculate the egg's acceleration. ....

    b)   How long did it take for the egg to reach a velocity of 40 m/s?

    ....

Q2   Below is a **velocity-time graph** for the descent of a **lunar lander**.
It accelerates due to the pull of gravity from the Moon.

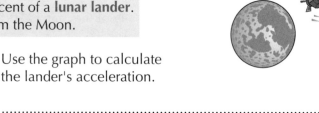

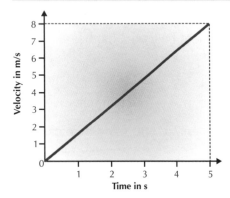

Use the graph to calculate
the lander's acceleration.

....

....

....

Q3   A car accelerates at **2 m/s²**. After **4 seconds** it reaches a speed of **24 m/s**.

    How fast was it going before it started to accelerate?

    ....

    ....

Q4   Describe the **type of motion** happening at each of the labelled points on the velocity-time graph.

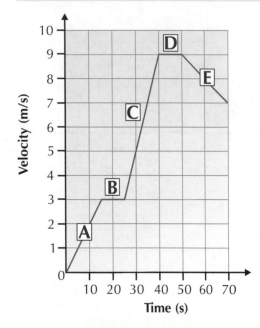

(A) ....

(B) ....

(C) ....

(D) ....

(E) ....

Forces

Q1   A bear rides a bike north at a constant speed.

a)   Label the forces acting on the bear.

....

....

b)   The bear brakes and slows down.
Are the forces balanced **as** he slows
down? If not, which direction is the
overall force in?

....

....

Q2   A teapot sits on a table.

a)   Explain why it **doesn't** sink into the table.

....

b)   Jane picks up the teapot and hangs it from the ceiling by a rope.
What vertical forces now act on the teapot?

....

c)   The rope breaks and the teapot accelerates towards the floor.

i)   Are the vertical forces balanced?

....

ii)   The teapot hits the floor without breaking and bounces upwards.
Which force causes the teapot to bounce upwards?

....

Q3   Samantha tests the **grip** of her favourite car tyre by dragging it across a **rough surface**.

Choose the correct options to complete her conclusions.

- When I first pulled it, the tyre didn't move.
  This showed that the forces acting on the tyre were in balance / unbalanced.

- When the tyre just started to move, the force I was pulling with was
  greater than / equal to the frictional force.

- While the tyre was moving with a steady speed, the force I was pulling with
  was greater than / equal to the frictional force.

Friction Forces and Terminal Velocity

Q1 Use the words below to complete the paragraph about a **skydiver**.

accelerates   decelerates   less   greater   decrease   balances   increase   constant

When a skydiver jumps out of a plane, his weight is .... than his air

resistance, so he .... downwards. This causes his air resistance to

.... until it .... his weight. At this point, his

velocity is .... When his parachute opens, his air resistance is

.... than his weight, so he .... This causes his air

resistance to .... until it .... his weight. Then his

velocity is .... once again.

Q2 Which of the following will **reduce** the drag force on an aeroplane?
Tick any appropriate boxes.

☐ flying higher (where the air is thinner)   ☐ carrying less cargo

☐ flying more slowly   ☐ making the plane more streamlined

Q3 A scientist plans to investigate **gravity** by dropping a hammer and a feather from a tall building.
Two onlookers predict what will happen. Say whether each is right or wrong, and explain why.

Paola: "They will land at the same time — gravity is the same for both."

Guiseppe: "The feather will reach its terminal velocity before the hammer."

a) Paola is **right / wrong** because ....

....

b) Guiseppe is **right / wrong** because ....

....

Q4 Mavis is investigating **drag** by dropping balls into a measuring cylinder
full of oil and timing how long they take to reach the bottom.
She does the experiment with a **golf ball**, a **glass marble** and a **ball bearing**.

From this experiment, can Mavis draw any conclusions about
the effect of size on drag? Explain your answer.

....

....

Friction Forces and Terminal Velocity

Q5 The graph shows how the **velocity** of a **skydiver** changes before and after he opens his parachute.

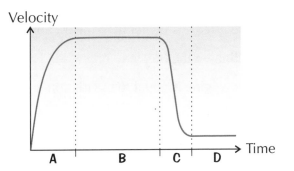

For each of the four regions A-D say whether the force of **weight** or **air resistance** is greater, or if they are **equal**.

	weight is greater	air resistance is greater	both equal
Region A:	☐	☐	☐
Region B:	☐	☐	☐
Region C:	☐	☐	☐
Region D:	☐	☐	☐

Q6 Two skydivers jump out of a plane. Kate opens her parachute after **3 seconds**, when she is still accelerating rapidly. Alison doesn't open her parachute yet but uses her video camera to film Kate's skydive. On the film Kate's parachute appears to pull her suddenly **upwards** when it opens.

a) Is Kate really moving upwards? Explain your answer. ....

....

b) Describe how Kate's velocity changes when her parachute opens. ....

....

Q7 On **Venus**, atmospheric pressure is about **90 times** that on Earth, but the gravitational field strength is about the same.
On **Mars**, atmospheric pressure is about **1/100th** of that on Earth and the gravitational field strength is less than half that on Earth.

Higher atmospheric pressure means the atmosphere is <u>thicker</u> and provides <u>more resistance</u>.

Probes which land on other planets often need parachutes to slow them down during their descent. What **size** of parachute would you recommend, relative to a parachute used on Earth, for:

a) landing on Venus: ....

b) landing on Mars: ....

Top Tips: When objects move through the air at high speed, the air resistance is proportional to the object's **velocity squared**. That's why, for skydivers, air resistance soon balances their weight and they reach terminal velocity. It's also why **driving** very fast is very **inefficient**.

Forces and Acceleration

Q1   Sue is driving the school bus at a **steady speed** along a straight level road.
Tick the boxes next to any of the following statements that are true.

☐ The driving force of the engine is bigger than the friction and air resistance combined.

☐ There are no forces acting on the bus.

☐ The driving force of the engine is equal to the friction and air resistance combined.

☐ No force is required to keep the bus moving.

Q2   State whether the forces acting on the following items are
balanced or **unbalanced**, and explain your reasoning.

a)   A **cricket ball** slowing down as it rolls along the outfield.

....

b)   A **car** going round a roundabout at a steady 30 mph.

....

c)   A **vase** knocked off a window ledge.

....

d)   A **satellite** orbiting over a fixed point on the Earth's surface.

....

e)   A **bag of rubbish** ejected from a spacecraft in empty space.

....

Q3   The table below shows the **masses** and **maximum accelerations** of four different antique cars.

Car	Mass (kg)	Maximum acceleration (m/s²)
Disraeli 9000	800	5
Palmerston 6i	1560	0.7
Heath TT	950	3
Asquith 380	790	2

Write down the names of the four cars in order of increasing driving force.

1. ....   2. ....

3. ....   4. ....

Forces and Acceleration

Q4 The diagram below shows the **forces** acting on an aeroplane.

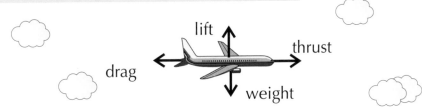

a) The aircraft is flying horizontally at a constant speed of 200 m/s. Which of the following statements about the aeroplane is true? Circle the appropriate letter.

    A   The thrust is bigger than the drag and the lift is bigger than the weight.

    B   The thrust is smaller than the drag and the lift is equal to the weight.

    C   The thrust is equal to the drag and the lift is bigger than the weight.

    D   The thrust is equal to the drag and the lift is equal to the weight.

b) What happens to the forces as the plane descends for landing and slows down to 100 m/s? Choose the correct options to complete the following statements:

i) The thrust is **greater than / less than / equal to** the drag.

ii) The lift is **greater than / less than / equal to** the weight.

Remember — the plane is losing height as well as slowing down.

Q5 Use the words supplied to fill in the blanks.

| proportional | force | reaction | stationary | accelerates | opposite |
| constant | resultant | inversely | balanced | | |

If the forces on an object are .... , it's either .... or moving at a .... speed.

If an object has a .... force acting on it, it .... in the direction of the .... The acceleration is .... to the force and .... to the mass.

For every action there is an equal and ....

Q6 A car tows a caravan along a road. At a **constant speed**, the pulling force of the car and the opposing reaction **force** of the caravan are **equal**. Which statement correctly describes the forces between the caravan and the car when the **car accelerates**? Tick the appropriate box.

    ☐ "The caravan's reaction force cancels out the pulling force of the car, so the caravan won't accelerate."

    ☐ "The caravan's reaction force is at a right angle to the force pulling the car, so the two forces don't affect one another."

    ☐ "The car's pulling force accelerates the caravan. The caravan's reaction force acts on the car, not the caravan."

Forces and Acceleration

Q7 Which picture shows the **weight (w)** and **reaction force (R)** of a car on a slope?
Tick the appropriate box.

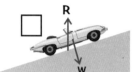 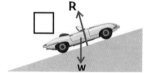 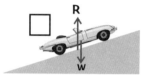 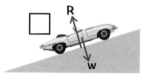

Q8 A very heavily laden **camper van** with a mass of **2500 kg** has a driving force
of **2900 N** and needs a force of **1500 N** to climb a hill at constant speed.
Would it be able to **overtake** a tractor which is accelerating at **0.6 m/s²**?
(Assume both vehicles are travelling at the same speed to begin with.)

....

....

Q9 Bill is hammering a nail into the wall.
The hammer hits the nail at a speed of **5 m/s** and takes **0.01 s** to stop.

a) What is the hammer's deceleration?

....

b) The mass of the hammer is 0.5 kg. Calculate the **force** the nail exerts on the hammer.

....

c) Complete the following force diagram.

i) Force of ....

on ....

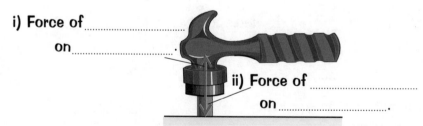

ii) Force of ....

on ....

Ben decides to have a go at hammering in the nail. He can only get the hammer up to a speed of
2.5 m/s rather than 5 m/s. The hammer also stops in 0.01 s.

d) Explain why Ben's hammering will exert a smaller force on the nail than Bill's.

....

....

Top Tips: Make sure that you learn the formula **F = m × a**. It really will be worth your
while, as without it you won't be able to calculate mass, acceleration or force in the exam.

Stopping Distances

Q1 **Stopping distance** and **braking distance** are **not** the same thing.

a) What is meant by 'braking distance'?

....

b) Use the words in the box to complete the following word equations.

braking	speed	reaction time	thinking

i) Thinking distance = ... × ....

ii) Stopping distance = ... distance + ... distance.

Q2 Will the following factors affect **thinking** distance, **braking** distance or **both**? Write them in the relevant columns of the table.

tiredness   road surface   weather   speed   diesel spills
alcohol   tyre tread   brakes   load   ice

Thinking Distance	Braking Distance

Q3 A car joins a motorway and changes speed from 30 mph to 60 mph. Which one of the following statements is **true**? Tick the appropriate box.

☐ Thinking distance will double and braking distance will more than double.

☐ Thinking distance will stay the same but braking distance will double.

☐ The total stopping distance will decrease.

Q4 A car has just been driven through a **deep puddle**, making the brakes wet. Explain why this will **increase** the **stopping distance** of the car.

....

....

P2 Topic 9 — As Fast As You Can

Car Safety

Q1   Circle the correct words or phrases to make the following statements **true**.

   a)   If the velocity of a moving object doubles, its **driving force** / **momentum** will double.

   b)   If you drop a suitcase out of a moving car, the car's momentum will **decrease** / **increase**.

   c)   When two objects collide the total momentum **changes** / **stays the same**.

   d)   When a force acts on an object its momentum **changes** / **stays the same**.

Q2   Calculate the **momentum** of a truck with a mass of 4500 kg that's travelling at 10 m/s.

   ....

Q3   A **750 kg car** is travelling at **30 m/s** along the motorway. It crashes into the barrier of the central reservation and is stopped in a period of **1.2 seconds**.

   a)   Find the size of the **average force** acting on the car as it stops.

   ....

   ....

   b)   Explain why the occupants of the car are likely to be less severely injured if they are wearing seatbelts made of slightly **stretchy** material.

   ....

   ....

Q4   The graph below shows the number of casualties from motorway traffic accidents in the country of Thornland.

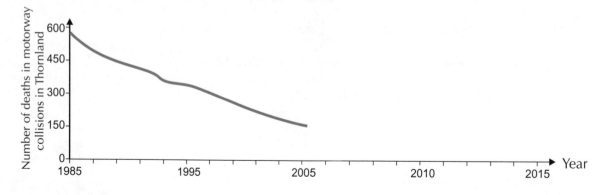

   a)   If the current trend continued, mark on the graph the point at which you would expect there to be **zero** casualties.

   b)   Explain why the trend is unlikely to continue in this way.

   ....

Taking Risks

Q1 The risk of my bus being late is **1 in 4**. Express this risk:

a) As a **fraction** .... b) As a **decimal** ....

c) As a **percentage** ....

Q2 Skydivers have a **reserve parachute** in case the main one fails.

a) Skydiving is a risky activity. Why do some people think it is worth the risk?

....

b) Suggest why having main **and** reserve parachutes reduces the risk of an accident.

....

Q3 Mr Burns is planning to build a new **power station**. The table shows the **risk** of four different types of power station **exploding** within 50 years.

Power Station	Risk of Explosion within 50 years
Coal	0.01
Oil	6/500
Nuclear	1.5%
Gas	0.014

An explosion would be a disaster — and cost Mr Burns loads of money. Which type of power station would you advise him to choose?

....

....

Q4 Some statistics have shown that **travelling by car** may be riskier than **travelling by plane**. Give two reasons why some people are happy to drive, but very scared of flying.

....

....

Q5 Susie and James are playing a board game using a six-sided dice. If they **roll a one**, they must miss the next turn.

a) Susie says the best way to work out the risk of rolling a one is just to use **probability**. Using her advice, what is the risk of rolling a one? Give your answer as a fraction.

....

b) James thinks the risk calculation should be based on **previous rolls** of the dice. James has rolled a one on two out of his last four turns. Using James' method, calculate the risk of rolling a one.

....

c) Whose method of risk assessment will give the most **accurate** answer? Give a reason for your answer.

....

Work and Kinetic Energy

Q1   Circle the correct words to make the following sentences true.

a)   Work involves the transfer of **force** / **heat** / **energy**.

b)   To do work **a force** / **an acceleration** must act over a **distance** / **time**.

c)   Work is measured in **watts** / **joules**.

Q2   Indicate whether the following statements are **true** or **false**.

		True	False
a)	Work is done when a toy car is pushed along the ground.	☐	☐
b)	No work is done if a force is applied to an object which does not move.	☐	☐
c)	Gravity does work on an apple that is not moving.	☐	☐
d)	Gravity does work on an apple that falls out of a tree.	☐	☐

Q3   An elephant exerts a constant force of **1200 N** to push a donkey along a track at a steady **1 m/s**.

a)   Calculate the work done by the elephant if the donkey moves **8 m**.

....

b)   From where does the elephant get the energy to do this work? ....

c)   Into what form(s) is this energy transferred when work is done on the donkey?

....

Q4   Ben's mass is 60 kg. He climbs a ladder. The rungs of the ladder are 20 cm apart.

a)   What force(s) is Ben doing work **against** as he climbs?

....

b)   As he climbs, what happens to the **energy** supplied by Ben's muscles?

....

....

20 cm

c)   How much work does Ben do when he climbs **10 rungs**? (Ignore any 'wasted' energy.)
Assume that g = 10 N/kg.

....

....

d)   How many rungs of the ladder must Ben climb before he has done **15 kJ** of work?
(Ignore any 'wasted' energy.) Assume that g = 10 N/kg.

....

....

Work and Kinetic Energy

Q5 Two tug-of-war teams compete to win a bunch of grapes. There are three men and two women in each team.

At the start of the contest, everyone pulls as hard as they can — the women can exert a force of 150 N each and the men can exert a force of 200 N each.

a) When everyone pulls with their maximum force, what is the work done by each team?

....

b) After a while, one of the men stumbles and falls over. Everyone else keeps pulling as hard as they can, but the other side manage to drag their opponents over the winning line — a distance of five metres. How much **work** have they done in order to win the grapes?

....

....

Q6 Find the **kinetic energy** of a 200 kg tiger running at a speed of 9 m/s.

....

....

Q7 A golf ball is hit and given 9 J of kinetic energy. The ball's velocity is 20 m/s. What is its **mass**?

....

....

....

Q8 A 60 kg skydiver jumps out of an aeroplane and free-falls. Find the skydiver's **speed** if she has 90 750 J of kinetic energy.

....

....

....

Top Tips: Work is done when a force makes things **move**. E.g. an Arctic explorer pulling a sledge over the ice exerts a **force** on the sledge which makes it **move** a certain **distance**. To get the sledge moving (from stationary), chemical energy from the explorer's food is transferred into kinetic energy (of the moving sledge) and into heat (because of friction between the sledge and the ice and in making the explorer a bit hot). Once the sledge is moving at a steady speed, energy is still being transferred — enough to keep on overcoming friction (and to keep our brave hero all hot and sweaty).

Electrical and Potential Energy

Q1   Dale loves a bit of DIY, and is drilling holes to put up some shelves.
His electric drill is attached to a **12 V** battery and uses a current of **2.3 A**.

   a)   Write down the equation that relates current, voltage, electrical energy and time.

....

   b)   If it takes Dale 30 seconds to drill one hole, how much energy
will be transformed by the motor if he drills **eight** holes?

....

....

Q2   Jerry was rescued from the sea by helicopter. He was lifted **10 m** using an electric motor.

   a)   Jerry weighs 70 kg. Calculate the **potential energy** he gained. (g = 10 N/kg)

....

   b)   The electric motor uses a voltage of 40 V and a current of 5 A.
Calculate how long the motor would take to transform the amount of energy that Jerry gained?

....

   c)   The motor would actually take much longer than this to lift Jerry. Explain why.

....

Q3   Fred works at a DIY shop. He has to load **28** flagstones onto the delivery truck.
Each flagstone has a mass of **25 kg** and has to be lifted **1.2 m** onto the truck.

   a)   How much gravitational potential energy does one flagstone
gain when lifted onto the truck? (g = 10 N/kg)

....

   b)   What is the **total gravitational potential energy** gained by the flagstones after they are all loaded
onto the truck?

....

   c)   How much **work** does Fred do loading the truck?

....

....

Conservation of Energy

Q1 The light bulb in this **torch** is powered by a battery.

a) What energy transformation is taking place in the battery?

.... energy to .... energy.

b) What energy transformations are taking place in the light bulb?

.... energy to .... energy and .... energy.

Q2 Mr Coles is about to demonstrate the **conservation of energy**.
He holds a heavy pendulum up by a window and lets go.

a) Explain why he can be sure that the pendulum won't smash the window when it swings back.

....

b) When the pendulum actually does swing back, it doesn't quite reach the height of the window again. Where has the potential energy gone?

....

Q3 Dave the frog **jumps** off the ground at a speed of 10 m/s.

a) If Dave has a mass of 500 g, what is his kinetic energy as he leaves the ground?

....

b) What is Dave's maximum possible potential energy?

....

c) What is the maximum height Dave can reach?

....

d) In practice, why won't Dave reach this height? (Explain your answer in terms of energy.)

....

Q4 Kim dives off a **5 m** high diving board and belly-flops into the swimming pool below.

a) If Kim's mass is 100 kg, calculate her kinetic energy as she hits the water.

....

b) At what speed will Kim be falling as she hits the water?

....

<u>*Power*</u>

Q1   Complete this passage by using the words provided.

heat	energy	100	rate	light	watts	joules

Power is the .... of doing work, or how much .... is

transferred per second. It is measured in .... or .... per

second.

A 100 W light bulb transfers .... joules of electrical energy into

.... and .... each second.

Q2   Catherine and Sally decide to run up a set of stairs to see who can get to the
top more quickly. Catherine has a mass of **46 kg** and Sally has a mass of **48 kg**. $g = 10 \text{ N/kg}$

a)   The top of the stairs is **5 m** above ground.
Calculate the gain in **potential energy** for:

i) Catherine ....

ii) Sally ....

b)   Catherine won the race in **6.2 s**, while Sally took **6.4 s**.
Which girl generated more **power**?

....

....

Q3   Tom likes to build model boats. His favourite boat
is the Carter, which has a motor power of **150 W**.

a)   How much **energy** does the Carter transfer in **10 minutes**?

....

b)   The petrol for the boat's motor can supply **30 kJ/ml**.
What volume of petrol is used up in **10 minutes**?

....

c)   Tom decides to get a model speed boat which transfers **120 kJ** in 10 minutes.
What is the **power** of the engine?

....

Top Tips: Power is a measure of the energy transferred, or work done, within a certain time
— the faster a person or machine can get a task done, the more powerful it is. Just think, if you were
a power-mad ruler you could try take over the world in the blink of an eye, mwah haa ha ha ha...

Circular Motion

Q1 Which of the following is the **best definition** of acceleration? Circle the appropriate letter.

A an increase in speed   **B** an increase in velocity   **C** a change in speed

D a change in direction   **E** a change in velocity

Q2 A **satellite** orbiting the Earth travels at a constant speed.

a) Is the satellite **accelerating**? Explain your answer.

....

b) Put a tick next to each **true** statement below.

☐ If a body is accelerating then there must be a resultant force acting on it.

☐ The forces acting on a body going round in a circle at a steady speed must be balanced.

☐ If there is no resultant force acting on a body then it carries on moving in a straight line at the same speed.

c) What is the general name for a force that keeps a body moving in a circular path?

....

d) Draw lines to match up the following bodies with the force that keeps them moving in a circle.

A runner running round a circular track	Gravity
A satellite in orbit round the Earth	Tension
The seats at the ends of the spokes of a spinning fairground ride	Friction

Q3 Circle the **correct** options in these sentences.

a) The greater the mass of a body, the smaller / **greater** the force needed to keep it moving in a circle.

b) It takes a greater force to keep a body moving in a **smaller** / larger circle.

c) A cyclist rides round a circular track at a speed of 20 m/s. The frictional force between his tyres and the track is 1467 N. He speeds up to 21 m/s — the frictional force changes to **1617 N** / 1331 N.

Q4 The diagram below shows a clock with hands that move **steadily** around the clock-face.

a) Draw and label with 'A' an arrow on the diagram to show the direction of the **velocity** of the tip of the **minute hand**.

b) Draw and label with 'B' an arrow to show the direction of the **acceleration** of the tip of the **hour hand**.

Circular Motion

Q5   The diagram below shows a car going round a roundabout.
The car is travelling at a **constant speed** of 10 m/s.

a)   Is the car **accelerating**? How do you know this?

....

....

b)   Draw an **arrow** on the diagram to show the direction
of the **force** acting on the car.

c)   The mass of the car is **1000 kg**. Calculate the size of
the force acting on the car.

....

....

d)   A **large truck** joins the roundabout. Would you expect the **centripetal force** acting on the truck to
be **larger** or **smaller** than the force acting on the car? Give a reason for your answer.

....

e)   It starts to **rain**. Why will the drivers not be able to drive as fast on the roundabout?

....

....

Q6   The Earth orbits the Sun because there is a **centripetal force** on it due to the Sun's gravity.
The size of this force is **3.6×10^{22} N.**

The radius of Earth's orbit around the Sun is 1.5×10^{11} m and the mass of the Earth is 6.0×10^{24} kg.

a)   Using the data above calculate the **speed** at which the Earth orbits the Sun.

....

b)   The diagram shows the Moon orbiting the
Earth due to the Earth's gravity. Use the information
on the diagram to calculate the **mass** of the Moon.

....

....

....

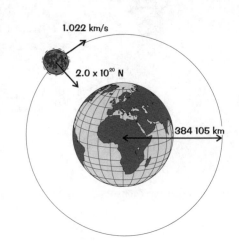

1.022 km/s

2.0×10^{20} N

384 105 km

Watch out for
changes of units.

Roller Coasters

Q1 A roller coaster and passengers are stationary at the top of a ride. At this point they have a gravitational potential energy of **300 kJ**. Each full carriage has a mass of 750 kg.

a) Draw lines to connect the correct energy statement with each stage of the roller coaster.

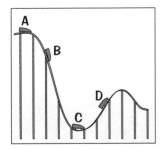

A   minimum P.E., maximum K.E.

B   K.E. is being converted to P.E.

C

D   maximum P.E.   P.E. is being converted to K.E.

K.E. = kinetic energy
P.E. = gravitational potential energy

b) **i)** When the roller coaster is at half its original height, how much **kinetic energy** should it have?

....

ii) Calculate the speed of each roller coaster carriage at this point.

....

iii) Explain why in real life the speed is **less** than this.

....

Q2 You have been asked to **design** a new roller coaster for a theme park.

a) Write down two **safety features** that you could include in your design.

....

b) Write down two benefits that your new ride could have for the **local community**.

....

Q3 On the 'Cliff Edge' roller coaster, the **1200 kg** carriages are **stopped** at the top of a huge vertical drop before being released. The roller coaster reaches a speed of **22 m/s** at the bottom of the drop before going into several loop-the-loops.

a) Calculate the height of the vertical drop.

....

....

b) What two forces act on you during the loop-the-loop? ....

c) Explain why you feel a lot lighter at the top of the loop than at the bottom.

....

__Einstein's Relativity__

Q1 Isaac and Albert are measuring the **speed of the light** produced from the headlights of a spaceship.

Isaac measures the speed of the light when the spaceship is **still**. He finds that the light is travelling towards him at **300 million m/s**.

Albert also measures the speed of the light, but this time the spaceship is **moving** towards him at a speed of **100 million m/s**.

If Albert measures everything correctly, then what **speed** does he measure?

....

Q2 The **theory of relativity** was developed in several stages. Rearrange the stages below in the correct order by numbering the boxes 1 to 7.

☐ Einstein began his famous thought experiments about light, time and space.

☐ Newton developed his laws of motion.

☐ The theory made very precise new predictions (e.g. about the effects of motion on time).

☐ Developments in technology enabled these predictions to be tested.

☐ Discovery that the speed of light is always the same can't be explained using Newton's laws.

☐ General acceptance of the theory of relativity.

☐ Einstein produced his theory of relativity.

Q3 The theory of relativity only predicted different results from **Newton's laws of motion** for objects moving at incredibly fast speeds or in incredibly strong gravitational fields.

a) Newton's laws were developed in the 17th century. Why did it take around **200 hundred years** before scientists realised that they were slightly wrong?

....

b) At everyday speeds and gravity, Einstein's theory predicts exactly the same results as Newton's. Explain why this is an important feature of Einstein's relativity and adds weight to the evidence that his theory is valid.

....

c) In some situations the two theories predicted different outcomes. Outline how this was tested using **atomic clocks**.

....

....

Einstein's Relativity

Q4   Many theories, like relativity, are based on **thought experiments**.

a)   What is meant by a "thought experiment"?

....

b)   Why are thought experiments extremely useful when creating new theories?

....

c)   Apart from experimental evidence, name a factor that would increase the chances of a theory being accepted.

Hint — Einstein was not the only scientist looking at the speed of light.

....

Q5   **Cosmic rays** can produce particles called muons.

a)   What happens to the lifetime of muons when they move close to the speed of light?

....

b)   Does this support or go against the prediction made by relativity? Explain your answer.

....

....

Q6   Some things predicted by relativity have not yet been observed.

a)   Explain why this doesn't prove that the theory of relativity is wrong.

....

b)   Scientific theories can never be proved right — they can only be proved wrong. Why is this?

....

....

c)   Why does the development of new **measuring instruments** sometimes lead to support for or against a scientific idea?

....

Top Tips: Many scientists like to think they know an awful lot about their subject, so if someone comes along with a radical new idea, it's often hard for them to accept it. Testing the new idea is a good way of helping people to believe it — if it predicts the right answer of course.
P.S. If you spot a gravity wave then tell everyone about it — just make sure you get a photo first.

Mixed Questions — P2 Topics 9 & 10

Q1   Norman loves trainspotting. As a special treat, he not only notes the train numbers but plots a **distance-time** graph for two of the trains.

a)   For how long is train 2 stationary?

....

b)   Both trains start at a steady speed.
How can you tell this from the graph?

....

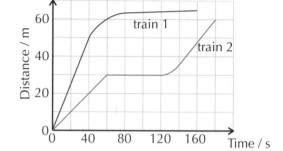

c)   Calculate the initial speed of the faster train.

....

d)   Describe the motion of train 1 between 40 s and 80 s.

....

Q2   In the film 'Crouching Sparrow, Hidden Beaver', a **95 kg** dummy is dropped **60 m** from the top of a building. (Assume that g = 10 m/s².)

a)   Sketch a distance-time graph and a velocity-time graph for the dummy from the moment it is dropped until just after it hits the ground.
(Ignore air resistance and assume the dummy does not reach a terminal speed.)

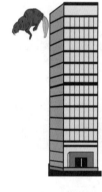

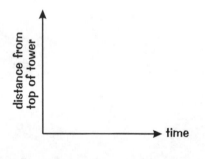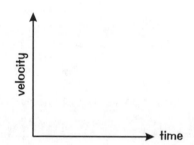

b)   Do any forces act on the dummy when it lies still on the ground (after falling)? If so, what are they?

....

c)   The take doesn't go to plan so the dummy is lifted back to the top of the building using a motor.

   i)   How much work is done on the dummy to get it to the top of the building?

   ....

   ii)   The useful power output of the motor is **760 W**.
   How long does it take to get the dummy to the top of the building?

   ....

   iii) If the motor uses the mains (**230 V**), calculate the current. (Assume it is 100% efficient.)

   ....

Mixed Questions — P2 Topics 9 & 10

Q3 Liz goes on a roller coaster. With her in it, the roller coaster carriage has a total mass of **1200 kg**.

a) What is the weight of the carriage? (Assume g = 10 m/s².)

....

b) At the start of the ride the carriage rises up to its highest point of **60 m** above the ground and stops. Calculate its gain in potential energy.

....

c) Write down the principle of the conservation of energy.

....

....

d) The carriage then falls to a third of its maximum height. Assuming there is no air resistance or friction, calculate the speed of the carriage at this point.

....

....

....

e) Along the way, the carriage does a loop-the-loop. Explain why Liz feels much heavier at the bottom of the loop than at the top.

....

....

f) At the end of the ride, the carriage slows down, decelerating at **6.4 m/s²**. How long does it take the carriage to slow down from **18 m/s** and come to a stop?

....

....

g) **i)** Write down one safety feature that should be installed on a roller coaster.

....

ii) Suggest two ways a new theme park would affect the surrounding community.

....

....

Mixed Questions — P2 Topics 9 & 10

Q4   A sky-diver jumps out of an aeroplane.
His weight is **700 N**.

a)   What force causes him to accelerate downwards?

....

b)   After **10 s** he is falling at a steady speed of **60 m/s**.
State the force of air resistance that is acting on him.

....

c)   He now opens his parachute, which increases the air resistance to **2000 N**.
Explain what happens immediately after he opens the parachute.

....

....

d)   After falling with his parachute open for **5 s**, the sky-diver is travelling at a steady speed of **4 m/s**.
What is the air resistance force now?

....

Q5   Dexter is scared of flying. He decides to take a risk and face his fear by
travelling on a high speed aeroplane with his favourite atomic clock.

a)   Write down two factors which influence a person's willingness to take risks.

1. ....

2. ....

b)   Trying not to think about flying, Dexter calculates the chance of getting a tasty aeroplane meal as
1/320 and decides not to risk it. Convert this fraction into a percentage.

....

c)   i)   How would the time on Dexter's clock be different from that on a stationary atomic clock?

....

ii)   What theory does this observation support?

....

iii)   Give one reason why it took so long for this theory to be accepted.

....

Mixed Questions — P2 Topics 9 & 10

Q6   Cherie and Tony rob a bank. They escape in a getaway car with a mass of **2100 kg** and travel at a constant speed of **90 km/h** along a straight, level road.

a)   Is there a resultant force on the car? Explain your answer.

....

b)   Calculate the momentum of the car.

....

c)   A police car swings into the middle of the road and stops ahead of Cherie's car. Cherie brakes with a reaction time of **0.7 s** and the car comes to a halt **3.0 s** after she hits the brakes.

   i)   Calculate her thinking distance.

   ....

   ii)   Write down one factor that could affect Cherie's thinking distance.

   ....

   iii)   Assuming the car decelerates uniformly, find the force acting on the braking car.

   ....

   ....

d)   Explain how seat belts would have helped keep Cherie and Tony safer if they had crashed.

....

Q7   The V-T graph below shows part of a car's journey round a racing track.

a)   Describe the motion of the car between:

   i)   40 s and 70 s ....

   ii)   100 s and 130 s ....

b)   Calculate how many metres the car travelled at 160 km/h.

....

....

c)   The car whizzes around a semicircular bend on the track with a radius of 180 m.
The car has a mass of 560 kg and is going at 38 m/s. Calculate the centripetal force on the car.

....

....

Ionising Radiation

Q1   Complete the passage using the words given below. You will not have to use all the words.

| ions | less | more | electrons | further | less far | protons |

When ionising radiation hits atoms, it sometimes knocks ....

off the atoms and makes them into .... Radiations that are

more ionising travel .... into a material and tend to cause

.... damage in the material they have penetrated.

Q2   Complete the table below by choosing the correct word from each column.

Radiation Type	Ionising power weak/moderate/ strong	Charge positive/none/ negative	Relative mass no mass/ small/large	Penetrating power low/moderate/ high	Relative speed slow/fast/ very fast
alpha					
beta					
gamma					

Q3 a)   For each sentence, tick the correct box to show whether it is **true** or **false**.

True False

i)   All nuclear radiation is positively charged.

ii) Gamma radiation has no mass because it is an EM wave.

iii) Alpha is the slowest and most strongly ionising type of radiation.

iv) Beta particles are electrons, so they do not come from the nucleus.

b)   For each of the false sentences, write out a correct version.

....

....

....

When Terry went to school they didn't teach him to avoid ionising radiation.

Ionising Radiation

Q4 Radiation from three sources — A, B and C — was directed towards target sheets of **paper**, **aluminium** and **lead**. Counters were used to detect where radiation passed through the target sheets.

Source A — the radiation was partially absorbed by the lead.
Source B — the radiation was stopped by the paper.
Source C — the radiation was stopped by the aluminium.

What type of radiation is emitted by:

    source A? ....,   source B? ....,   source C? ....

Q5 Explain clearly why gamma rays are **less ionising** than alpha particles.

....

....

....

Q6 Write down the atomic number and mass number for each type of radiation.

a) alpha   atomic number = ...   mass number = ...

b) beta   atomic number = ...   mass number = ...

c) gamma   atomic number = ...   mass number = ...

Q7 X-rays and gamma rays are electromagnetic waves.

a) Describe how gamma rays are released.

....

b) How are X-rays produced?

....

Top Tips: Alpha, beta and gamma radiation all have different properties, but there's a nice predictable relationship between those properties. So make sure you know, for example, the relationship between relative mass and penetrating ability — one increases while the other decreases. It's the same kind of thing for relative mass and speed.

P2 Topic 11 — Putting Radiation to Use

Background Radiation

Q1   Which of the following are **true**? Circle the appropriate letters.

    A About half of the UK's background radiation comes from radon gas.

    B The nuclear industry is responsible for about 10% of background radiation in the UK.

    C If there were no radioactive substances on Earth, there would be no background radiation.

Q2   The level of background radiation varies from place to place. For each of the following, indicate whether the background level will be **higher** or **lower** than average and explain your answer.

    a) In an aeroplane at high altitude, the level will be **higher** / **lower** than average because:

    ....

    b) In a mine, the level will usually be **higher** / **lower** than average because:

    ....

    c) In houses built above granite rocks, the level will usually be **higher** / **lower** than average because:

    ....

Q3   Peter did an experiment to compare equal quantities of two radioactive materials.
Here are his results and conclusion:

Material tested	Radiation measured (counts per second)
None	50
Material A	200
Material B	400

CONCLUSION
"Both materials are radioactive.
Material B is twice as radioactive
as Material A."

Is Peter's conclusion correct? Give a reason for your answer.

....

....

Q4   The concentration of **radon** gas found in people's homes varies across the UK.

    a) Why does the concentration vary across the country?

    ....

    b) Explain why high concentrations of radon are dangerous.

    ....

    c) How can people in high radon areas reduce the radon concentration in their homes?

    ....

Atomic Structure

Q1   Fill in the blanks using the words below. Each word should be used only once.

radiation   isotope   element   protons   neutrons   nuclei   radioactive

Isotopes are atoms which have the same number of .... but different

numbers of .... Some isotopes are .... Their

.... are unstable, so they break down and spit out ....

When this happens the nucleus often changes into a new ....

Q2   Indicate whether these sentences are **true** or **false**.

                                                                      True False

a)   The nucleus of an atom takes up almost no space compared to the whole atom.   ☐ ☐

b)   Most of an atom's mass is in the electrons.   ☐ ☐

c)   Atoms of the same element with the same number of neutrons are called isotopes.   ☐ ☐

d)   Radioactive decay speeds up at higher temperatures.   ☐ ☐

Q3   The diagram shows uranium-238 decaying into thorium by alpha and gamma emission.

a)   Does the **gamma ray** emission have an effect on the nucleus? If so, what is it?

....

b)   Write the full nuclear equation for this decay, clearly showing the atomic and mass numbers.

....

Q4   Write the nuclear equations for the following decay processes.

a)   An atom of thorium-234 ($^{234}_{90}$Th) emits a beta particle and a gamma ray and becomes an atom of protactinium.

....

b)   An atom of radon-222 ($^{222}_{86}$Rn) emits an alpha particle and becomes an atom of polonium.

....

P2 Topic 11 — Putting Radiation to Use

Half-Life

Q1   A radioactive isotope has a half-life of **60 years**.
Which of these statements describes this isotope correctly? Tick one box only.

In 60 years, half of the atoms in the material will have gone. ☐

In 30 years' time, only half the atoms will be radioactive. ☐

In 60 years' time, the count rate will be half what it is now. ☐

In about 180 years there will be almost no radioactivity left in the material. ☐

Q2   Sandra measures how the radioactivity of a sample changes with time.
The table shows some of her results.

Time (minutes)	0	10	20	30	40	80	160
Counts per minute	740	553	420	326	260	140	103

a)   Use Sandra's results to draw a graph of counts per
minute against time.

b)   The counts per minute will never fall below 100.
Suggest two reasons why.

....

....

c)   Sandra calculates that the half-life of her sample is
about 20 minutes. Explain how she worked this
out. (You may find it useful to show some of the
working on your graph.)

Count rate (cpm)

....

....

Q3   The graph shows how the count rate of a radioactive isotope declines with time.

a)   What is the half-life of this isotope?

....

b)   What was the count rate after 3 half-lives?

....

c)   What fraction of the original radioactive nuclei will still be unstable after 5 half-lives?

....

d)   After how long was the count rate down to 100? ....

Half-Life

Q4 The half-life of uranium-238 is **4500 million** years. The half-life of carbon-14 is **5730** years.

a) What do the "238" in "uranium-238" and the "14" in "carbon-14" mean?

....

....

b) If you start with a sample of each element and the two samples have equal activity, which will lose its radioactivity most quickly? Circle the correct answer.

uranium-238   carbon-14

Q5 A radioactive isotope has a half-life of **40 seconds**.

You'll need to change 6 minutes into seconds.

a) What fraction of the unstable nuclei will still be radioactive after 6 minutes?

....

....

b) i) If the initial count rate of the sample was 8000 counts per minute, what would be the approximate count rate after 6 minutes?

....

....

ii) After how many whole **minutes** would the count rate have fallen below 10 counts per minute?

....

....

Q6 Peter was trying to explain half-life to his little brother. He said, "isotopes with a long half-life are always more dangerous than those with a short half-life."

Is Peter right? Explain your answer.

....

....

....

Top Tips: Half-life tells you **how quickly** a source becomes **less radioactive**. If your source has a half-life of 50 years then after 100 years the count rate will be 1/4 of its original value. But if the half-life's 10 years, after 100 years the count rate will be less than 1/1000th of its original value.

P2 Topic 11 — Putting Radiation to Use

Uses of Ionising Radiation

Q1 Complete the following paragraphs on radiotherapy using the words provided.

ill centre normal kill cells focused cancer dose radiotherapy

High doses of gamma radiation will .... living ....

Because of this, gamma radiation is used to treat .... This is called

....

Gamma rays are .... on the tumour using a wide beam. Damage to

.... cells can make the patient feel very .... This damage

is minimised by directing the radiation at the tumour and using the minimum

.... possible.

Q2 The table shows some commonly used radioisotopes and the type of radiation they emit.

a) Which of these isotopes would be most suitable for these applications?

Radioisotope	Decays by...
strontium-90	beta emission
americium-241	mainly alpha emission
cobalt-60	beta and gamma emission

   i) A smoke detector

   ....

   ii) To sterilise pre-packed food

   ....

b) What further information about these isotopes would you want before you considered using them?

....

Q3 The following sentences explain how a smoke detector works, but they are in the wrong order.

Put them in order by labelling them 1 (first) to 6 (last).

☐ The circuit is broken so no current flows.

[1] The radioactive source emits alpha particles.

☐ A current flows between the electrodes — the alarm stays off.

☐ The alarm sounds.

☐ The air between the electrodes is ionised by the alpha particles.

☐ A fire starts and smoke particles absorb the alpha radiation.

Uses of Ionising Radiation

Q4 The diagram shows how radiation can be used to sterilise surgical instruments.

radioactive source

thick lead

a) What kind of radioactive source is used, and why? In your answer, mention the **type** of radiation emitted (α, β and γ) and the **half-life** of the source.

....

....

b) What is the purpose of the thick lead?

....

Q5 Iodine-131 is commonly used as a tracer in medicine.

a) Normal iodine has a mass number of 127. Why is it no good as a tracer?

....

b) The thyroid gland normally absorbs iodine. Describe how iodine-131 can be used to detect if the thyroid gland is working properly.

....

....

....

Q6 A patient has a radioactive source injected into her body to test her kidneys.

A healthy kidney will get rid of the radioactive material quickly (to the bladder). Damaged kidneys take longer to do this.

The results of the test, for both the patient's kidneys, are shown opposite.

Kidney A

Kidney B

Count Rate / Time

Count Rate / Time

a) Explain how the doctor knew which kidney was working well and which was not.

....

....

b) Explain why an alpha source would **not** be suitable for this investigation.

....

....

144

Radioactive Dating

Q1   Carbon-14 makes up about 1/10 000 000 of the carbon in the air.

   a)   Name one gas in the air which contains carbon.

   ....

   b)   What proportion of the carbon present in organisms alive now is carbon-14?

   ....

   c)   What happens to the level of carbon-14 in a plant or animal after it dies?

   ....

Q2   A wooden spoon from an archaeological dig was found to have 1 part C-14 to 80 000 000 parts
   carbon. Work out when the wood was **living material**. (The half-life of C-14 is 5730 years.)

   ....

Q3   Uranium-238 has a half-life of 4.5 billion years.

   a)   Explain how the decay of uranium can be used to date rocks.

   ....

   ....

Rock, 243 019 yrs,
but young at heart.
Cumbria based, GSOH.
Likes: the outdoors.
Dislikes: dogs, moss

Mal
45,
seek
cur\
foot
mor

   b)   A meteorite contains uranium-238 and lead-206 in a ratio of 1:3. How old is the meteorite?

   ....

Q4   A leather strap was found to have 1 part C-14 in 320 000 000 parts C-12.

   a)   How many half-lives have occurred since the strap was a piece of skin on a living cow?

   ....

   The half-life of C-14
   is 5730 years

   b)   How old would this make the strap?

   ....

   c)   Explain how you could use a computer to reduce the error in measuring the strap's radioactivity.

   ....

   ....

P2 Topic 11 — Putting Radiation to Use

Radioactive Dating

Q5 Professor Zuton is trying to discover the age of a Roman soldier's uniform discovered in boggy ground. He thinks it must be around 1800 years old. To find out if he's right, he uses carbon dating to test different parts of the uniform. Here are his results and notes.

Item	Age according to C-14 dating (years)	Notes
Leather belt	1800	
Woollen jacket	1200	This must be wrong. It should be older than that.
Wooden button	2100	This is older than I was expecting...

I don't really care how old it is, I just wanted some free clothes...

The professor is sure all the parts are about the same age. List four reasons why the test results might disagree.

1. ....

2. ....

3. ....

4. ....

Q6 a) Read the following conversation and decide if everyone is right or wrong.

                                                                     True   **False**

    i) Amy — 'You can use carbon dating to find the age of any old coins you dig up.'   ☐   ☐

    ii) Katherine — 'Only if they're younger than 11 460 years. That's two half-lives. After that they have no carbon-14 left so they don't change any more.'   ☐   ☐

    iii) Laurence — 'If you use a computer to cut out experimental errors you can get the age spot-on every time.'   ☐   ☐

b) For each statement that was wrong, explain why.

....

....

....

....

....

....

Radioactivity Safety

Q1   Two scientists are handling samples of radioactive material.

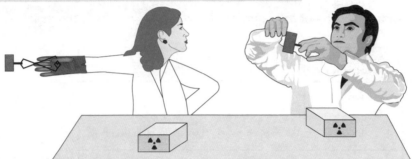

a)   One of the scientists is taking sensible safety precautions, but the other is not.
Describe three things which the careless scientist is doing wrong.

1. ....

2. ....

3. ....

b)   Describe another way the scientists can reduce their exposure to the radiation,
without using special apparatus or clothing.

....

c)   How should radioactive samples be stored when they are not in use?

....

Q2   The three different types of radiation can all be dangerous.

a)   Which **two** types of radiation can pass through the human body?
Circle the correct answers.

        alpha   beta   gamma

b)   i)   Which type of radiation is usually most dangerous if it's inhaled or swallowed?

....

ii)   What effects can this type of radiation have on the human body?

....

....

....

Top Tips: You should always handle radioactive sources really carefully. People who work
with radioisotopes often wear **dosimeters** — badges which record their exposure. We're all exposed
to a low level of **background radiation** every day, though — from rocks etc. — and you can't do
anything about that (unless you fancy wearing a lead-lined suit and breathing apparatus all day long.)

Splitting the Atom

Q1 Choose from the words below to complete the following passage.
You may need to use some words more than once.

| chemical | energy | relativity | fission | mass | equivalence | fusion |

In his theory of special ...., Einstein suggested that .... is

a form of ...., which can be converted into other forms of energy. This is

known as the principle of mass-energy .... Over 30 years later he was

proved right with the development of nuclear .... When a nucleus splits,

some of the .... is converted into a huge amount of ....

— much more than you would expect from a .... process.

Q2 Nuclear power is an example of how nuclear fission can be used **peacefully**.

a) Give one **destructive** use of nuclear fission. ....

b) How is the chain reaction different in this case compared to in a reactor?

....

Q3 Many nuclear power stations split **uranium** nuclei in their reactors.

a) Why are slow-moving neutrons fired at the uranium nuclei?

....

b) Each time a uranium atom splits, two or three neutrons are produced.
Describe how this leads to a chain reaction.

....

....

Q4 The **daughter nuclei** produced by fission are themselves **radioactive**.

a) What do the daughter nuclei do to become more stable?

....

b) Complete the following decay series for ^{91}Kr.

^{91}Kr ➡ .... ➡ .... ➡ .... ➡ ^{91}Zr

Nuclear Power

Q1 The diagram below shows how energy from a gas-cooled nuclear reactor generates electricity.

a) Describe how heat energy from the reactor is used to generate electricity.

....

....

b) What causes the reactor to get hot?

....

c) **i)** Explain how the control rods control the rate of fission.

....

....

ii) What material are control rods usually made from? ....

Q2 The majority of the UK's electricity is still produced by burning **fossil fuels**.

a) Write down one advantage and one disadvantage of nuclear power compared to using fossil fuels to generate electricity.

Advantage ....

Disadvantage ....

b) Describe how building a nuclear power plant can have a positive impact on its surrounding area.

....

Q3 **Radioactive waste** left over from **nuclear fission** is very difficult to dispose of.

a) Why is the waste produced by nuclear power stations such a long-term problem?

....

b) Describe one way of disposing of radioactive waste.

....

....

Nuclear Fusion

Q1 Decide whether the following statements are **true** or **false**.
Write out the correct version of any false statements.

True False

a) Nuclear fusion involves small nuclei joining together.

b) A nuclear fission reaction releases more energy than a nuclear fusion reaction.

c) Fusion reactors produce lots of radioactive waste.

d) Only a few experimental fusion reactors are generating electricity.

....

....

....

Q2 The energy released in stars comes from fusion.

a) Write down two conditions needed for fusion to take place.

1. ....   2. ....

b) Fusion reactors like JET are extremely hard to build.

i) Why can the hydrogen used not be held in a physical container?

....

ii) How do fusion reactors get around this problem?

....

c) Describe the main problem with the amount of energy a fusion reactor needs to operate.

....

Q3 In 1989 two scientists claimed to have created energy through **cold fusion**.

a) In what ways did they say cold fusion was different from previous ideas about nuclear fusion?

....

b) Suggest a reason why the report caused such excitement.

....

c) Explain why some scientists accepted the idea of cold fusion whilst others didn't.

....

....

Static Electricity

Q1 Fill in the **gaps** in these sentences with the words below.

electrons	positive	static	friction	insulating	negative

.... electricity can build up when two .... materials

are rubbed together. The .... moves .... from one

material onto the other. This leaves a .... charge on one of the

materials and a .... charge on the other.

Q2 **Circle** the pairs of charges that would attract each other and **underline** those that would repel.

positive and positive   positive and negative   negative and positive   negative and negative

Q3 The sentences below are wrong. Write out a **correct** version for each.

a) A polythene rod becomes negatively charged when rubbed with a duster because it loses electrons.

....

....

b) A charged polythene rod will repel small pieces of positively charged paper if they are placed near it.

....

....

c) The closer two charged objects are together, the less strongly they attract or repel.

....

....

d) If a positively charged object is connected to earth by a metal strap, electrons flow through the strap from the object to the ground, and the object is safely discharged.

....

....

e) Build-up of static can cause sparks if the distance between the object and the earth is big enough.

....

....

Static Electricity

Q4 A **Van de Graaff generator** is a machine which is used to generate static electricity. One type of Van de Graaff generator works like this:

1. The bottom comb is positively charged and attracts electrons away from the rubber belt.

2. The rubber belt loses electrons and becomes positively charged.

3. As the positive charge on the belt passes the top comb, electrons are attracted from the metal dome onto the belt.

4. The dome loses electrons and builds up a positive charge.

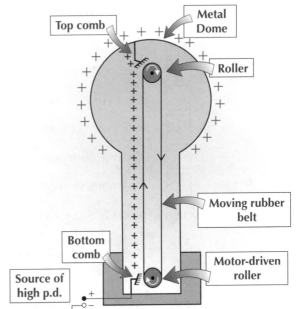

a) The top comb needs to be a **conductor**. Explain why.

....

....

b) Nadia is doing an experiment with a Van de Graaff generator. Her teacher tells her that if she touches the generator, she will become charged. When Nadia touches the generator, her hair starts to stand on end.

Use your knowledge of electrostatic charges to **explain why** Nadia's hair stands on end.

....

....

Q5 As Peter switched off his TV, he noticed that the screen was dusty. When he wiped it with his finger he heard a **crackling** sound and felt a slight **electric shock**.

Peter made two statements about what happened. Give a **reason** why he said each of the following:

a) *"The screen must have been at a high voltage."*

....

....

b) *"When I touched it, part of the screen was discharged to earth."*

....

....

Top Tips: In the exam, remember to talk about electrons flowing from one place to another. The positive charges don't move — static electricity is always due to the movement of **electrons**.

Static Electricity — Examples

Q1   Forensic scientists use an **electrostatic dust-lifter** to take fingerprints at a crime scene.

a)   Use the number boxes to put the following list into the right order.

☐   Dust particles are attracted to the thin film.

☐   A thin film is given a high positive charge.

1   Fine dust is brushed over the fingerprint.

☐   The thin film is pressed onto the fingerprint.

☐   An impression of the fingerprint is left on the film.

b)   Write down two other uses for an electrostatic dust-lifter.

1. ....   2. ....

Q2   Use the words below to fill in the gaps.

fuel	earth	fuel tanker	sparks	explosion	metal strap

Static electricity can be dangerous when refuelling aircraft. If too much static builds up, there

might be ...., which can set fire to the ....

This could lead to a huge .... To prevent this happening, the fuel tank

can be connected to .... with a .... so that the

charge is conducted away. Alternatively, connect the .... to the plane.

Q3   Match up these phrases to describe what happens in a **thunderstorm**.
Write out your complete sentences below in the correct order.

If the voltage gets big enough...

... the voltage gets higher and higher.

The bottoms of the clouds become negatively charged...

... and electrons are transferred between them.

As the charge increases...

... there is a huge spark (a flash of lightning).

Raindrops and ice bump together...

... because they gain extra electrons.

1. ....

2. ....

3. ....

4. ....

Static Electricity — Examples

Q4   All of these statements about laser printing are wrong.   Write a **corrected version** of each.

a)   Under the control of a computer, the laser scans across the uncharged rotating drum and gives parts of it a positive charge, creating an image on the drum.

....
....
....

b)   The toner used in a laser printer is not charged, so it will only stick to parts of the drum which are positively charged.

....
....

c)   The drum rolls over an uncharged piece of paper, and the powder is attracted to the paper which picks up the image.

....
....
....

d)   The paper then passes through the fuser which presses the image firmly into the paper making a permanent print.

....

Q5   Three friends are talking about **static electricity**.

Why do some of my clothes get charged up during the day?

Do cotton clothes get charged as much as nylon clothes?

How come I get zapped by my car door every time I get out?

Lisa

Tim

Sara

Answer their questions in the spaces below.

Lisa: ....
....

Sara: ....
....

Tim: ....
....

Top Tips: Static electricity's responsible for many of life's little annoyances — bad hair days, and those little shocks you get from touching car doors and even stroking the cat. Still, it has its uses too — the main ones you need to know about are **fingerprinting** and **laser printing**.

Mixed Questions — P2 Topics 11 & 12

Q1 The table gives information about four different **radioisotopes**.

a) Explain how the atomic structure of cobalt-60 is different from the structure of 'normal' cobalt-59.

....

....

Source	Type of Radiation	Half-life
radon-222	alpha	3.8 days
technetium-99m	gamma	6 hours
americium-241	alpha	432 years
cobalt-60	beta and gamma	5.27 years

b) Which sources in the table would be most suitable for each of the uses below?

medical tracers   smoke detectors   detecting leaks in pipes

....

c) Radiation can be used to treat cancer.

i) What type of radiation is used in this treatment? ....

ii) Explain why patients often feel very ill while receiving this treatment.

....

d) Jim measures the count rate of a sample of americium-241 as 120 cpm.
Roughly how long would it take for the count rate to fall below **4 cpm**? Show your working.

....

....

e) Give one precaution Jim should take while handling the radioactive sample.

....

Q2 Approximately **one in 10 000 000** of the carbon atoms found in living plants or animals are atoms of the radioactive isotope **carbon-14**. After a plant or animal dies this proportion starts to decrease. Carbon-14 has a **half-life** of **5730** years.

a) Calculate the fraction of the atoms in a pure sample of carbon-14 that will still **not** have decayed after 10 half-lives have gone by.

....

....

b) Approximately how old is a bone fragment in which the proportion of carbon-14 is one part in 50 000 000? Explain your answer.

....

....

Mixed Questions — P2 Topics 11 & 12

Q3   The diagram below shows part of a chain reaction in a nuclear reactor.

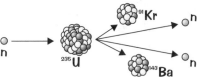

a)   What is the name of the type of radioactive decay shown in the diagram? ....

b)   This decay happens as part of a chain reaction. Describe what happens in this chain reaction.

....

....

c)   The daughter nuclei produced are radioactive.

     i)   Describe how they become stable.

....

     ii)   Write down the decay series for ^{143}Ba.

....

d)   How is the rate of the chain reaction controlled in a reactor?

....

e)   What would happen if this reaction was not controlled?

....

f)   Describe how thermal energy from the reactor is used to generate electricity.

....

....

g)   Give one disadvantage of using nuclear power compared to using fossil fuels.

....

Nuclear **fusion** produces more energy than the process above.

h)   **i)**   Write down one of the conditions needed for fusion to take place.

....

     ii)   Some scientists claim to have produced energy through cold fusion.
         Explain why the theory has not been accepted by the scientific community.

....

....

Mixed Questions — P2 Topics 11 & 12

Q4 The diagram shows an aircraft being refuelled.
No safety precautions have been taken.

a) **i)** Explain how static electricity could cause an explosion in this situation.

....

....

ii) Give one precaution that can be taken to avoid this danger.

....

b) Write down one example of how static electricity is **useful**.

....

Q5 Fay measures the count rate of a sample of pure copper-64 in her home,
using a Geiger counter. The graph below shows her results.

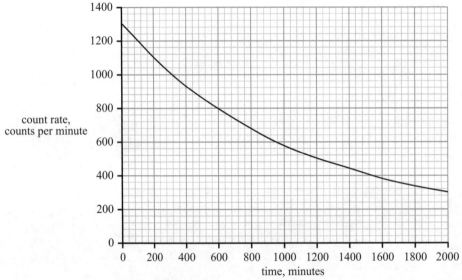

a) Fay had previously measured the background rate to be 100 counts per minute.
Find the half-life of copper-64.

....

b) She takes her Geiger counter to her friend's house and finds the background rate is much higher.
Give one reason why background radiation changes from place to place.

....

c) Her friend explains that she lives in a high **radon** area.

i) What disease is her friend more at risk of developing? ....

ii) How could she reduce the concentration of radon in her house?

....

P2 Topic 12 — Power of the Atom